COOKBOOK

COOKBOOK

60 CRACKING CADBURY CREME EGG RECIPES

HarperCollins*Publishers*

A SERVING OF THE RECIPES IN THIS BOOK SHOULD BE SEEN AS AN INDULGENT TREAT, BEST ENJOYED ONLY OCCASIONALLY. IT IS IMPORTANT TO FOLLOW A HEALTHY BALANCED DIET AND ACTIVE LIFESTYLE.

NONE OF THESE RECIPES ARE SUITABLE FOR MILK OR DAIRY ALLERGY SUFFERERS. IF YOU DO SUFFER WITH AN ALLERGY, PLEASE CHECK THE INGREDIENTS LIST ON EACH RECIPE.

HarperCollins*Publishers*
1 London Bridge Street
London SE1 9GF
www.harpercollins.co.uk

First published by HarperCollins*Publishers* 2020

10 9 8 7 6 5 4 3

Recipes created by Jayne Cross with the following exceptions: p86, p89, p92 by Liam Charles; p22, p23, p48, p50, p114 by Martha Collison; p51, p107 by ELVIS; p33, p40, p84, p85 by Georgia Green of Georgia's Cakes; p26, p32, p120 by Georgia Levy; p27, p122, p123 by Natalie Thomson.

Photography by Steve Lee
Food styling by Jayne Cross
Prop styling by Jo Harris
Design by Sim Greenaway

A catalogue record of this book is available from the British Library

ISBN 978-0-00-835687-3

Printed and bound in Great Britain by Bell and Bain Ltd, Glasgow

CONTENTS

INTRODUCTION

IT'S TIME TO GET EGGSPERIMENTAL, BECAUSE YOUR CADBURY CREME EGG PRAYERS HAVE BEEN ANSWERED!

From profiteroles to pavlovas, from brownies to breads, we've found a way to pop a Cadbury Creme Egg into pretty much every deliciously indulgent sweet or savoury snack you can think of. Packed with 60 delicious new ways to enjoy these gorgeously gooey goodies, this cracking cookbook offers tasty treats that are right up everyone's street.

So what are you waiting for? It's time to satisfy that sweet tooth and get creative in the kitchen with Cadbury Creme Eggs.

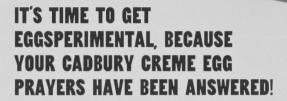

CADBURY CREME EGG MILLIONAIRE'S SHORTBREAD

Ridiculously rich and gorgeously gooey, you won't be short-changed by these shortbread bites! It'll be hard not to eat them all in one sitting.

MAKES 20 PIECES
PREP TIME 40 MINS *(circled) ~ 2hr ~ nope*
COOKING TIME 15 MINS

FOR THE SHORTBREAD
75g caster sugar
150g butter
225g plain flour

FOR THE CARAMEL LAYER
100g butter
50g golden syrup
150g caster sugar
1 x 397g can condensed milk

FOR THE CHOCOLATE TOPPING
100g dark chocolate, broken into small pieces
50g milk chocolate, broken into small pieces
2 Cadbury Creme Eggs, chopped into pieces

Per serving

308 kcals	14.8g fat	9.2g sat fat	31.4g sugar	0.08g salt

1. Preheat the oven to 180°C/160°C fan/gas mark 4 and line an 18 x 28cm baking tin with non-stick baking parchment.
2. To make the shortbread, cream together the sugar and butter until pale and fluffy, then add the flour and mix to form a soft dough. Tip into the baking tin and spread it out with your fingertips to cover the base of the tin in an even layer.
3. Bake the shortbread in the oven for 15 minutes until it is golden, then remove it and set it aside to cool.
4. Next make the caramel. Put all the ingredients into a medium saucepan and heat them gently until the butter has melted and the sugar dissolved, stirring occasionally. Increase the heat and bring the caramel to the boil, stirring frequently, allowing it to bubble for 5–10 minutes until the sauce thickens and turns a golden caramel colour.
5. Pour the caramel on to the shortbread and smooth into an even layer. Put the tin in the fridge until the caramel is set.
6. To make the chocolate topping, melt the dark and milk chocolate in a bowl in the microwave or over a pan of gently simmering water. When the mixture is completely smooth pour it over the caramel layer, tapping the tin on the work surface so the melted chocolate settles in an even layer.
7. Top with the Cadbury Creme Egg pieces and use the tip of a knife to gently swirl the pieces into the chocolate topping.
8. Leave the shortbread to cool completely before cutting it into squares with a sharp knife.

leave to cool before putting in fridge – then leave in fridge for at least few hours. obviously

CADBURY CREME EGG CHELSEA BUNS

These little beauties are bunbelievable! There's not much that beats a hot sticky bun fresh from the oven. Pair it with a seriously strong cuppa. Photographed overleaf.

MAKES 12
PREP TIME 30 MINS,
PLUS 1 HOUR PROVING
COOKING TIME 25 MINS

FOR THE DOUGH

250ml skimmed milk
75g butter
7g fast-action yeast
450g strong white flour
45g caster sugar
1 tsp salt
1 egg, lightly beaten

FOR THE FILLING

50ml double cream
25g butter
2 Cadbury Creme Eggs, chopped
60g chopped hazelnuts (optional)

1. Heat the milk in a small pan until it is lukewarm, then add the butter to melt it. Pour the mixture into a jug, sprinkle over the yeast and whisk lightly.

2. Mix the flour, sugar and salt in a large bowl, then add the warmed milk mixture and half the beaten egg. Stir with a wooden spoon until the mixture starts to come together, then tip it on to a floured surface and knead it until it forms a soft, slightly sticky dough – you might need to add a little more flour. Knead for 10 minutes until you have a soft and smooth dough.

3. Put the dough into a lightly oiled bowl, cover it with a clean tea towel and leave it in a warm place to rise for about 30 minutes, or until it has doubled in size.

4. Meanwhile make the filling. Heat the cream, butter and one of the chopped Cadbury Creme Eggs in a small pan until the chocolate starts to melt and the mixture begins to bubble. Remove the pan from the heat, whisk the mixture until it is smooth and pour it into a bowl. Leave it to cool. Line a deep 20 x 25cm baking tin with baking parchment.

Per serving

213 kcals	9.4g fat	5g sat fat	9.4g sugar	0.6g salt

5. Once the dough has risen, tip it out on to a floured surface, knead it again lightly, then roll it out into a 30 x 40cm rectangle. Spread the Cadbury Creme Egg filling evenly over the dough and sprinkle the hazelnuts on top, if using. Starting from a long edge, roll up the dough tightly to form a long sausage. With a large sharp knife, cut it into 12 even-sized pieces and put them in the baking tin. Cover them with a tea towel and leave them to rise for 20 minutes.

6. Preheat the oven to 200°C/180°C fan/gas mark 6. Brush the buns with the remaining beaten egg then bake them in the oven for 20–25 minutes, or until they are golden brown. Remove the tin from the oven and immediately dot the top of the buns with the remaining Cadbury Creme Egg pieces.

7. Leave the buns to cool slightly, then remove them from the tin and serve – they are best served warm.

TIP If you want to serve these fresh from the oven for breakfast, put the covered baking tin with the rolled buns in the fridge overnight (before the second rising). Remove the tin from the fridge 45 minutes before baking for the second rising.

CADBURY CREME EGG DIPPED MADELEINES

Tuck into these magnificent madeleines. Buttery, fluffy and with a rich Cadbury Creme Egg sauce, you could dip for days!

MAKES 18
PREP TIME 25 MINS
COOKING TIME 10 MINS

130g butter, melted and cooled
120g caster sugar
2 eggs
120g plain flour

FOR THE DIPPING SAUCE
2 Cadbury Creme Eggs, chopped into pieces
2 tbsp runny honey
2 tbsp double cream

You will need two madeleine tins

1. Preheat the oven to 220°C/200°C fan/gas mark 7 and butter the madeleine tins with a little of the melted butter.
2. Whisk the sugar and eggs in a large bowl with a hand-held whisk for 8–10 minutes until the mixture is very pale and thick. Add a third of the flour and fold it into the egg mixture, then add the remaining two-thirds of the flour. Pour the cooled butter into the bowl and fold it in until fully incorporated.
3. Spoon a tablespoon of the mixture into each of the madeleine moulds in the tin, then bake them in the oven for 8–10 minutes until they are risen and golden brown. Remove the cakes from the tin immediately and leave them to cool for 10 minutes on a wire rack.
4. Meanwhile make the Cadbury Creme Egg dipping sauce by heating the Cadbury Creme Egg pieces, honey and cream in a small pan over a gentle heat. Whisk the mixture until it is smooth, then remove the pan from the heat and pour the sauce into a small bowl.
5. Serve the madeleines with the dipping sauce alongside.

Per serving

140 kcals	8g fat	4.5g sat fat	11g sugar	0.05g salt

CADBURY CREME EGG DODGERS

You'll want to try this delicious biscuit. Hard on the outside, but crack it open and it's gooey in the middle. No one'll be dodging this dessert! Photographed overleaf.

MAKES 10
PREP TIME 30 MINS
COOKING TIME 15 MINS

FOR THE BISCUITS

150g self-raising flour
50g plain flour
125g caster sugar
125g butter, diced
50g cocoa powder
1 egg, lightly beaten
1 tsp vanilla extract

FOR THE BUTTERCREAM

40g butter, softened
75g icing sugar
½ tsp milk
1 Cadbury Mini Creme Egg, chopped into pieces

FOR THE DRIZZLE (OPTIONAL)

100g icing sugar
yellow food colouring

You will need two different-sized egg-shaped cutters

Per serving

305 kcals	15g fat	9.5g sat fat	21g sugar	0.2g salt

1. Preheat the oven to 180°C/160°C fan/gas mark 4 and line two baking sheets with baking parchment.
2. Put the self-raising flour, plain flour and sugar into a food processor and whizz briefly to combine. Add the butter and mix again until the mixture resembles fine breadcrumbs.
3. Add the cocoa powder, egg and vanilla extract and pulse until the mixture starts to come together.
4. Tip the mixture on to a lightly floured surface and gently knead it together to form a smooth dough.
5. Roll out the dough to the thickness of a £1 coin, then cut out egg shapes using a 9 x 7cm egg-shaped cookie cutter and place them on the baking sheets. Use a smaller egg-shaped cutter to cut egg shapes from the centre of half the cookies. Alternatively, cut out the small holes by hand.
6. Roll together the scraps of dough and continue to cut out shapes until you have 20 cookies in total.
7. Bake the cookies in the oven for 15–18 minutes until they are crisp and have darkened slightly. Remove them from the baking sheets and leave them to cool on wire racks.

8. To make the buttercream, beat the butter with a hand-held electric whisk, then gradually add the sugar, beating well between each addition until the mixture is soft and smooth. Add the milk with the last of the sugar. Add the Cadbury Creme Egg pieces and fold them into the buttercream.

9. Spread the buttercream on the whole egg cookies, then top each one with a cookie which has a hole in the centre.

10. To make the drizzle, if using, put the icing sugar into small bowl and add 1½–2 tablespoons cold water and mix until you have an icing with a thick drizzling consistency. Colour half of the icing yellow and then spoon both into small piping bags. Snip the end off the bags and then drizzle both over the filled cookies in a zigzag pattern and leave to set for an hour. The cookies will keep for a week stored in an airtight container.

TIP You can make these cookies to decorate an Easter twig tree. Make a small hole in the top of each cookie before baking them. Don't fill them with buttercream, but decorate them with more drizzle or fondant icing then thread a piece of ribbon through each hole, tie the ribbon into loops and hang them from a twig tree.

CADBURY CREME EGG CARAMEL SHORTBREAD BITES

You should never be in short supply of these deliciously different bite-sized biscuits. A great gooey twist on Granny's secret recipe!

MAKES 56
PREP TIME 30 MINS,
PLUS COOLING
COOKING TIME
20–25 MINS

FOR THE SHORTBREAD
250g plain flour
50g caster sugar
175g butter, cubed

FOR THE CARAMEL
1 x 397g can condensed milk
100g soft light brown sugar
150g butter
1 tsp sea salt

FOR THE CHOCOLATE TOPPING
5 Cadbury Creme Eggs, chilled
200g dark chocolate, broken into small pieces

1. Preheat the oven to 180°C/160°C fan/gas mark 4. Grease and line a 20cm square tin with baking parchment.
2. To make the shortbread base, combine the flour and sugar in a large bowl. Add the chunks of butter and use your fingertips to rub it into the dry ingredients until the mixture resembles breadcrumbs. Press the mixture into the tin and bake it for 20–25 minutes, or until pale golden.
3. While the shortbread is cooking make the caramel layer. Put the condensed milk, sugar and butter in a large saucepan. Cook over a medium heat for about 5–7 minutes, stirring all the time so the mixture doesn't burn on the bottom, until it turns a dark golden brown and thickens slightly. Stir in the salt then pour the mixture over the shortbread base.
4. Cut the Cadbury Creme Eggs in half and arrange the halves over the caramel. Press them in gently, leaving about 1cm sticking out of the caramel. Leave to set for at least 1 hour.
5. Melt the chocolate over a pan of boiling water (making sure that the bottom of the bowl does not touch the water) or in the microwave, and then carefully pour it over the caramel shortbread. Do not pour it directly on to the Cadbury Creme Egg pieces as you want them to remain visible. Spread the chocolate around the eggs and leave it to set completely before slicing.

Per serving

127 kcals	7g fat	4.3g sat fat	11g sugar	0.1g salt

CADBURY CREME EGG ZESTY BARS

Raise the bar with these zesty little fridge fillers. Crunchy biscuit base, orange filling and crushed Cadbury Creme Egg drizzle all make for a treat that's bound to keep your taste buds on their toes.

MAKES 35
PREP TIME 20 MINS,
PLUS COOLING
COOKING TIME 10–15 MINS

FOR THE BASE
100g digestive biscuits
2 tbsp cocoa powder
2 tbsp butter, melted

FOR THE CURD
2 tbsp cornflour
150g caster sugar
4 eggs
2 egg yolks
250ml freshly squeezed orange juice
zest of 2 oranges
85g butter, cubed

FOR THE CADBURY CREME EGG DRIZZLE
1 Cadbury Creme Egg, crushed
2 tbsp double cream

1. Line a 23cm square baking tin with baking parchment, covering both the base and sides. Preheat the oven to 170°C/150°C fan/gas mark 3.
2. Blend the digestive biscuits and cocoa powder in a food processor until fine crumbs form. Pour in the melted butter and pulse until the mixture starts to come together. Press the mixture into the base of the tin.
3. To make the curd, whisk together the cornflour, sugar, eggs, yolks, orange juice and zest in a large saucepan. Stir in the cubes of butter, and then put over a low heat. Whisk the mixture continuously until the butter melts and the curd thickens slightly – about 5 minutes.
4. When the mixture is thick enough to coat the back of a spoon, pour it over the base. Use a spatula to smooth the top and then bake it for 10–15 minutes. There should be a slight wobble in the centre when you take the tin out of the oven. Allow it to cool completely at room temperature, then put it in the fridge.
5. To make the drizzle, put the crushed Cadbury Creme Egg and cream into a small heatproof bowl over a pan of boiling water. Heat, stirring all the time, until the egg is fully melted and a thick chocolate sauce has formed. Drizzle over the cooled mixture with a spoon.
6. When the drizzle has set, cut the mixture into bars and serve. Store in the fridge.

Per serving

78 kcals	4.5g fat	2.5g sat fat	6g sugar	0.06g salt

CADBURY CREME EGG DUFFINS

Cadbury Creme Egg Duffins will have all your guests stuffin' their faces. This incredible culinary combo of Cadbury Creme Egg, doughnut and muffin with its sweet, sugary outer and gooey chocolatey middle is the dessert of dreams.

MAKES 12
PREP TIME 20 MINS
COOKING TIME 18 MINS

125g butter, melted and cooled, plus extra for greasing

350g self-raising flour

175g caster sugar

2 eggs

150ml buttermilk

3 Cadbury Creme Eggs, cut into quarters

FOR THE SUGAR COATING

75g granulated sugar

½ tsp ground cinnamon

25g butter, melted

You will need a 12-hole muffin tin

1. Preheat the oven to 190°C/170°C fan/gas mark 5 and butter the holes of the muffin tin.
2. Put the flour and caster sugar in a large bowl. Whisk together the cooled, melted butter, the eggs and the buttermilk in a jug until they are combined. Add this to the bowl and stir gently until the cake batter is just mixed – don't overwork it or the cakes won't be light and fluffy.
3. Spoon a dessertspoon of batter into each muffin tin hole, add a Cadbury Creme Egg quarter to each, then top with another spoonful of batter, ensuring that each Cadbury Creme Egg piece is completely covered.
4. Bake the duffins in the oven for 16–18 minutes until they are well risen and golden. While they are cooking mix the sugar and cinnamon in a shallow bowl.
5. Take the muffin tin out of the oven and leave the duffins to cool for a couple of minutes, then remove them from the tin, brush each one with a little melted butter and coat it with the cinnamon sugar. Leave them to cool completely on a wire rack. These are best eaten on the day they are baked.

Per serving

344 kcals	12.5g fat	7.7g sat fat	28.6g sugar	0.3g salt

 TIP You can substitute 150ml of low fat natural yoghurt mixed with 1 tablespoon of lemon juice for the buttermilk in this recipe.

CADBURY CREME EGG S'MORES

Gather round the campfire and try our gooey take on these all-American treats. Quick, easy and guaranteed to taste better when eaten while listening to scary stories.

MAKES 6
PREP TIME 1 MIN

3 Cadbury Creme Eggs, halved
6 marshmallows
12 light digestive biscuits

1. Place the halved Cadbury Creme Eggs on a plate and microwave them on a medium–high heat for 10 seconds until they are softened but still hold their shape.
2. Place the marshmallows on skewers (two per skewer) and heat them briefly under a grill until they expand and turn golden brown.
3. Divide the digestives between six plates and place half a softened Cadbury Creme Egg on six of the biscuits and a toasted marshmallow on the other six. Spread out each marshmallow to cover a whole biscuit.
4. To serve, put the digestives together in a sandwich and squeeze them slightly, but try not to squeeze out the centres.

Per serving

243 kcals	7.2g fat	2.25g sat fat	23g sugar	0.5g salt

CADBURY CREME EGG COOKIES

You'll go cuckoo for these cookies! Everyone eggspects chocolate chips, but try mixing them up with melt-in-your-mouth Cadbury Creme Eggs and watch these delicious little cookies fly off the plate.

MAKES 12
PREP TIME 10 MINS
COOKING TIME 8 MINS

75g unsalted butter
60g soft light brown sugar
60g caster sugar
1 egg, beaten
½ tsp vanilla extract
150g self-raising flour
¼ tsp salt
50g dark chocolate, roughly chopped
6 Cadbury Mini Creme Eggs, halved
25g icing sugar
orange gel food colouring

1. Preheat the oven to 180°C/160°C fan/gas mark 4. Line a large baking sheet with baking parchment.
2. Put the butter and sugars in a bowl and beat with a hand-held whisk until light and fluffy. Add the beaten egg and vanilla extract and beat the mixture again to combine everything.
3. Sift in the flour and salt and mix them in to form a stiff dough. Add the chocolate pieces then divide the dough into 12 balls. Spread them well apart on the baking sheet and bake them in the oven for 4 minutes.
4. Take the cookies out of the oven and place half a Cadbury Mini Creme Egg on top of each one, then return them to the oven for a further 4 minutes. Remove the cookies from the oven and allow them to cool a little.
5. While the cookies are in the oven make the icing by mixing the icing sugar with a little water until you have a slightly stiff but still runny consistency. Put half the mixture in another bowl and add a little food colouring.
6. Using two spoons lightly drizzle the white icing over the top of each cookie, then repeat with the orange icing. Allow the icing to set before eating.

Per serving

192 kcals	7.8g fat	4.5g sat fat	18g sugar	0.2g salt

CADBURY CREME EGG FLAPJACKS

Don't get into a flap if you're feeling a bit peckish, our Cadbury Creme Egg flapjack is the perfect snack. So indulgent and rich you won't look back.

MAKES 20
PREP TIME 15 MINS
COOKING TIME 30 MINS

200g butter
175g golden syrup
100g soft light brown sugar
250g jumbo oats
100g plain flour
1 Cadbury Creme Egg, cut into small pieces

FOR THE TOPPING (OPTIONAL)
60g white chocolate
yellow food colouring

1. Preheat the oven to 170°C/150°C fan/gas mark 3 and grease and line a shallow 20 x 30cm baking tin with baking parchment.
2. Heat the butter, golden syrup and sugar in a pan over a gentle heat, stirring until everything has melted. Put the oats and flour in a bowl, pour over the melted butter mixture, stir well, then spoon it into the prepared baking tin.
3. Dot the Cadbury Creme Egg pieces over the top, pushing them into the oats slightly.
4. Bake the flapjack in the oven for 25–30 minutes until it is golden and set. Remove the tin from the oven and leave it to cool for 10 minutes, then remove the flapjack from the tin and allow it to cool for an hour on a wire rack.
5. To make the topping, if using, melt the chocolate in a microwave on a medium heat, or in a bowl set over a pan of gently simmering water. Drizzle half of it over the flapjack, then colour the other half with a little yellow food colouring and drizzle again, criss-crossing the white drizzle.
6. Leave the chocolate to set before cutting the flapjack into squares. They will keep for up to a week in an airtight container.

Per serving

195 kcals	10g fat	5.5g sat fat	13.3g sugar	0.03g salt

CADBURY CREME EGG FONDANT FANCIES

Who isn't fond of a fondant fancy? Give these sweet treats a Cadbury Creme Egg twist by hiding bits of gooey goodies inside. You can thank us later.

MAKES 25
PREP TIME 30 MINS,
PLUS COOLING AND SETTING
COOKING TIME 30 MINS

FOR THE SPONGE

225g butter, softened
225g caster sugar
4 eggs, lightly beaten
2 tsp vanilla extract
225g self-raising flour

FOR THE TOPPING

600g fondant icing sugar
2 tbsp cocoa powder
4¼ Cadbury Creme Eggs, cut into 25 pieces
100g icing sugar
yellow food colouring

You will need two small piping bags and two wire racks

Per serving

289 kcals	9.5g fat	5.6g sat fat	40g sugar	0.07g salt

1. Preheat the oven to 180°C/160°C fan/gas mark 4, then grease and line a 20cm square 5cm deep baking tin with non-stick baking parchment.
2. Put the butter and sugar in a large bowl and beat them with a hand-held electric mixer until you have a pale, thick mixture. Add the eggs a little at a time, beating well between each addition, adding the vanilla extract with the last of the egg.
3. Fold in the flour then spoon the mixture into the baking tin, smoothing the surface with the back of a spoon.
4. Bake in the oven for 25–30 minutes until the sponge looks golden brown and a skewer inserted in the centre comes out clean. Leave it to cool in the tin for 10 minutes, then turn out the sponge on to a wire rack to cool completely.
5. Cut the sponge into 25 squares, put them back on the wire rack and chill them for 1–2 hours, or ideally overnight. This firms the sponge pieces and makes it easier to ice them.
6. To make the topping mix the fondant icing sugar and cocoa powder together in a large bowl, add 100ml cold water and beat the mixture with a wooden spoon until it is smooth. Add a little extra water if you need to; the mixture should be thick, but runny enough to coat the cakes.
7. Put two wire racks over two large baking sheets. Take one of the sponge squares and spread the sides with icing using a small round-bladed knife, then put the cake on one of the wire racks. Repeat with the rest of the cake squares.
8. Top each cake with a piece of Cadbury Creme Egg, then put a spoonful of icing on top of each, ensuring that you cover

the egg completely as well as the top of the cake so the icing starts to drizzle down the sides. This gives the top of the cake a smooth finish. Repeat with the remaining squares, then leave them for a couple of hours to set completely.

9. Once the fondant icing has set, put the icing sugar in a bowl and mix it with a little cold water to make a thick, runny icing. Spoon half the icing into another bowl and add a little yellow food colouring. Spoon the icing into two small piping bags, snip off the ends and then drizzle both over all the cakes.

10. Leave the cakes to set for another hour before serving. They will keep for 2–3 days in an airtight container.

CADBURY CREME EGG FOREST FRIDGE CAKE

This easy-to-make creation is cooled to perfection and bound to have the masses begging for more. So grab your Cadbury Mini Creme Eggs and stock up your kitchen with your new favourite fridge cake.

MAKES 20 SQUARES
PREP TIME 10 MINS,
PLUS 2 HOURS CHILLING

50g unsalted butter, cut into small pieces

225g dark chocolate, broken into small pieces

20ml golden syrup

150g rich tea biscuits, crushed

75g dried apricots, finely chopped

75g seedless raisins, finely chopped

30g roasted chopped hazelnuts, crushed

10 Cadbury Mini Creme Eggs, halved

1. Line a 20 x 25cm deep baking tin with baking parchment.
2. Put the butter and chocolate in a bowl and microwave them on medium–high for about 2 minutes until they are melted. Alternatively put them in a heatproof bowl over a saucepan of gently simmering water and heat for 2–3 minutes, stirring occasionally, until they are melted.
3. Stir in the golden syrup, biscuits, apricots, raisins and hazelnuts and mix them together well with a spoon.
4. Press the mixture into the tin with a wooden spoon, then push in the Cadbury Mini Creme Egg halves, spacing them evenly.
5. Chill in the fridge for at least 2 hours until set.
6. Slice the cake into 20 squares and store it in the fridge until you are ready to eat.

Per serving

168 kcals	8.3g fat	3.8g sat fat	16g sugar	0.2g salt

CADBURY CREME EGG MACARONS

What have macarons always been missing? Bite into one of these
and find out. They're rich, crunchy and – thanks to their
special ingredient – gorgeously gooey.

MAKES 24
PREP TIME 2 HOURS
COOKING TIME 10–12 MINS

65g ground almonds

125g icing sugar

10g cocoa powder, plus extra
for dusting

2 large egg whites

100g caster sugar

100ml single cream

100g dark chocolate, broken into
pieces

4 Cadbury Creme Eggs

You will need a piping bag with a
round nozzle

1. Sift together the ground almonds, icing sugar and cocoa
   powder into a bowl.
2. Put the egg whites into another bowl and whisk them with a
   hand-held whisk, gradually adding the caster sugar, until stiff
   peaks form. Fold the egg white into the dry mixture a third at
   a time.
3. Fill a piping bag with a round nozzle. Line a baking tray with
   baking parchment and pipe £2 coin-sized circles on to the
   parchment, leaving a 2cm gap between each. Leave them for
   20 minutes until a skin forms.
4. Preheat the oven to 120°C/100°C fan/gas mark 1. Dust the
   macarons with a little cocoa powder making a slight pattern
   on the surface and bake them for 10–12 minutes.
5. To make the ganache filling heat the cream in a small
   saucepan over a low heat. Pour it over the chocolate pieces
   in a heatproof bowl, then stir until the chocolate has melted.
   Leave it to cool and thicken, stirring occasionally.
6. Remove the cooked macaron shells from the oven and allow
   them to cool completely before taking them off the tray.
7. Heat a sharp knife in hot water and slice the Cadbury Creme
   Eggs widthways into 5–6 circular pieces. Fill a piping bag
   with the ganache filling. Arrange the macaron shells in pairs.
   Place a slice of Cadbury Creme Egg in the centre of one shell
   and pipe a ring of ganache around it. Sandwich another shell
   on top to form the macaron. Continue until you have paired
   up all the macaron shells.

Per serving

116 kcals	4.5g fat	2g sat fat	16.5g sugar	0.02g salt

CADBURY CREME EGG & BEETROOT BROWNIES

Yes, you read that right. If you're up for a bit of eggsperimental baking, you'll struggle to beat these bad boys. Incredibly tasty and deliciously light, these Cadbury Creme Egg and beetroot brownies will make you the talk of the table.

MAKES 20
PREP TIME 20 MINS
COOKING TIME 30 MINS

225g dark chocolate, broken into pieces

150g butter

225g golden caster sugar

3 eggs

120g plain flour

200g cooked beetroot, grated

3 Cadbury Creme Eggs, cut into 20 pieces

1. Preheat the oven to 180°C/160°C fan/gas mark 4. Butter and line a 20 x 30 x 4cm baking tin with baking parchment.
2. Place the chocolate and butter in a bowl and melt in a microwave or over a saucepan of gently simmering water. Stir the mixture until it is smooth and then set it aside to cool.
3. Whisk the sugar and eggs in a large bowl with a hand-held whisk until the mixture is pale and thick. Whisk the cooled chocolate and butter into the eggs, then gently fold in the flour and grated beetroot until everything is evenly mixed. Pour the mixture into the tin.
4. Dot the Cadbury Creme Egg pieces on top of the batter, spacing them so that each brownie will have a piece of Cadbury Creme Egg on it.
5. Bake in the oven for 25–30 minutes until the brownie is firm to the touch. Leave it to cool in the tin for 10 minutes, then place it on a wire rack to cool completely before cutting it into 20 pieces. The brownies will keep for up to a week in an airtight container.

Per serving

220 kcals	11g fat	6.5g sat fat	22g sugar	0.07g salt

CADBURY CREME EGG BANANA BREAD

It's time we brought Nana's banana bread back from the brink by smothering it in ridiculously delicious Cadbury Creme Egg buttercream. Best served in eggstremely thick slices!

SERVES 12
PREP TIME 30 MINS
COOKING TIME 1 HOUR

FOR THE BANANA BREAD

120g butter, softened, plus extra for greasing
175g soft light brown sugar
2 eggs, lightly beaten
1 tsp vanilla extract
150g self-raising flour
100g wholemeal flour
3 very ripe bananas
75ml low-fat natural yoghurt
1 Cadbury Creme Egg, chopped into pieces

FOR THE BUTTERCREAM (OPTIONAL)

75g butter, softened
2 Cadbury Creme Eggs, chopped into pieces
125g icing sugar
1 tbsp milk

1. Preheat the oven to 180°C/160°C fan/gas mark 4, then butter and line a 900g loaf tin with baking parchment.
2. In a large bowl beat the butter and sugar with a hand-held electric whisk until they are pale and thick. Add the egg a little at a time, beating well with each addition and adding the vanilla extract with the last bit of egg.
3. Fold in the flours then peel the bananas and mash them with the yoghurt. Add this to the bowl with the chopped Cadbury Creme Egg and fold everything in until it is evenly mixed. Pour the mixture into the tin and bake it in the oven for an hour until it is golden brown and a skewer inserted in the middle comes out clean. Check it after 50 minutes and cover the top with a piece of foil if it is too brown.
4. Remove the tin from the oven and leave the bread to cool in the tin for 10 minutes, then remove the loaf and allow it to cool completely on a wire rack.
5. To make the buttercream, if using, melt 25g of the butter in a small pan with the Cadbury Creme Egg pieces, then set it aside to cool. Beat the remaining butter with a hand-held mixer until it is soft, then add the icing sugar along with the melted Cadbury Creme Egg mixture. Beat again until the mixture is smooth. You might need to add a tablespoon of milk for a smooth consistency. Spread the buttercream over the top of the banana bread, cut it into slices and serve.

Per serving

232 kcals	7g fat	3.9g sat fat	20.6g sugar	0.17g salt

GOOEY CADBURY CREME EGG CAKE

For a fresh take on cake, try this recipe. It has layer upon layer of gooey goodness, decorated with loads more Cadbury Creme Eggs, so do be sure to share. This recipe is a very tasty but indulgent treat, best enjoyed on special occasions.

SERVES 16
PREP TIME 1 HOUR 30 MINS
COOKING TIME 30–40 MINS

FOR THE CAKE
250g butter
250g caster sugar
4 eggs
225g self-raising flour
25g cocoa powder
1 tsp vanilla bean paste

FOR THE BUTTERCREAM
425g icing sugar
75g cocoa powder
150g softened butter
60ml skimmed milk

TO DECORATE
50ml single cream
40g dark chocolate, broken into pieces
2 Cadbury Creme Eggs, chopped into pieces

You will need two 15cm cake tins

Per serving

487 kcals	25.3g fat	15.4g sat fat	47.3g sugar	0.2g salt

1. Preheat the oven to 180°C/160°fan/gas mark 6 and line the cake tins with baking parchment.
2. In a small saucepan melt the butter over a low heat then pour it over the sugar in a large bowl. Add the eggs and mix them through, then the flour, cocoa powder and vanilla bean paste. Mix until everything is incorporated.
3. Divide the mixture equally between the cake tins and bake them for 30–40 minutes until the cakes are cooked through.
4. To make the buttercream, beat together the icing sugar, cocoa powder, butter and milk using a hand-held whisk. Keep beating until the mixture is light and fluffy.
5. Level the top of each cake and cut both in half so you have four equal layers.
6. Spread a layer of buttercream on top of one layer and place the second layer on top. Repeat with the second and third layer. For the fourth, make sure the top layer is facing down so you have the flattest side on the top. Add the last layer and encase the whole cake with buttercream. Scrape off any excess with a scraper and palette knife and chill the cake in the fridge until the buttercream is firm.
7. To decorate the cake, heat the cream in a small saucepan then pour it over the chocolate in a bowl and mix until the chocolate has melted. Pour the mixture over the cake and push it towards the edges with a palette knife, letting it gently drip down the sides. Use any leftover buttercream to stick pieces of Cadbury Creme Egg to the top of the cake before serving.

CADBURY CREME EGG TOPPED GINGER LOAF

If you thought nothing could top a ginger loaf you'd be wrong!
This Cadbury Creme Egg topped ginger loaf is the best thing ever.

SERVES 12
PREP TIME 25 MINS
COOKING TIME 1 HOUR

120g butter
120g demerara sugar
120g golden syrup
100g black treacle
225g plain flour
1 tsp bicarbonate of soda
1 tsp ground ginger
1 tsp mixed spice
2 eggs, lightly beaten
50ml milk

FOR THE TOPPING

50ml whipping cream
2 Cadbury Creme Eggs,
chopped into pieces

1. Preheat the oven to 160°C/140°C fan/gas mark 2 and grease and line a 900g loaf tin with baking parchment.
2. Put the butter, sugar, syrup and treacle in a saucepan and heat them gently until the butter melts and the sugar crystals dissolve.
3. Sift the dry ingredients into a large bowl, add the contents of the pan and beat the mixture well. Add the eggs and milk and beat again until you have a smooth thick batter. Pour this into the tin and bake the loaf for 1 hour until it is firm to the touch and a skewer inserted in the middle comes out clean.
4. Leave the loaf to cool in the tin for 10 minutes, then turn it out on to a wire rack and leave it to cool completely.
5. To make the topping, heat the cream and two of the chopped Cadbury Creme Eggs in a small saucepan until the chocolate starts to melt and the mixture begins to bubble. Remove the pan from the heat, whisk the mixture until it is smooth, pour it into a bowl and leave it to cool.
6. Spread the cooled topping on top of the loaf, allowing it to drizzle down the sides. Decorate it with the remaining Cadbury Creme Egg pieces. Leave the topping to set before slicing and serving the loaf – it will keep for up to a week in an airtight container.

Per serving

294 kcals	12g fat	7g sat fat	28g sugar	1g salt

CADBURY CREME EGG CHOCOLATE ROULADE

This swish roll will go down an absolute treat. So rich and so creamy it's a dream come true! And it's easy to freeze too, so you can save some for later (if you really want to).

SERVES 10
PREP TIME 30 MINS
COOKING TIME 15 MINS

icing sugar or cocoa for dusting

FOR THE SPONGE
6 eggs
175g caster sugar
175g plain chocolate, melted and cooled

FOR THE DRIZZLE (OPTIONAL)
25ml double cream
1 Cadbury Creme Egg, chopped into small pieces

FOR THE FILLING
250ml double cream
2 Cadbury Creme Eggs, chopped

1. Preheat the oven to 200°C/180°C fan/gas mark 6 and grease a 20 x 30cm Swiss roll tin, then line the base with baking parchment.
2. To make the sponge, put the eggs and sugar in a large bowl and whisk them for about 5 minutes with a hand-held mixer until the mixture becomes very pale and thick and leaves a ribbon trail when you lift the mixer from the bowl.
3. Gently fold in the cooled chocolate then spoon the mixture into the tin, spreading it into the corners and smoothing the top as you go. Bake in the oven until it is firm to the touch and starting to shrink away from the edges, about 15 minutes.
4. Remove the tin from the oven, cover it with a clean tea towel and place it on a wire rack. Leave the sponge to cool completely while it is still in the tin.
5. Make the chocolate drizzle, if using, by heating the cream and the Cadbury Creme Egg pieces in a small saucepan until the chocolate starts to melt and the mixture begins to bubble. Remove from the heat, whisk the mixture until it is smooth, then pour it into a bowl and leave it to cool.
6. Whip the cream for the filling in a large bowl until you have soft peaks, then gently fold in the chopped Cadbury Creme Eggs.

Per serving

245 kcals	10g fat	5g sat fat	32g sugar	0.14g salt

7. Turn the cooled sponge on to a sheet of baking parchment and spread the whipped cream over it, stopping 1cm from the edges. Starting from a short edge roll up the sponge using the sheet of baking parchment to help you. Place the rolled sponge on a serving plate with the end of the roll underneath and drizzle over the chocolate sauce, if using, or dust with icing sugar or cocoa. Cut the roulade into slices and serve.

CADBURY CREME EGG & PASSION FRUIT CHOCOLATE LAYER CAKE

This mouth-watering dessert will re-eggnite your passion for the humble layer cake. Sweet, sharp, rich – the Cadbury Creme Egg topping is the literal icing on the cake! Photographed overleaf.

SERVES 18
PREP TIME 30 MINS
COOKING TIME 30 MINS

FOR THE SPONGE

300g butter, softened
300g golden caster sugar
5 eggs, lightly beaten
2 tsp vanilla extract
360g self-raising flour
1 tsp bicarbonate of soda
60g cocoa powder
300ml low-fat buttermilk
150g dark chocolate, melted and cooled

FOR THE TOPPING

50ml single cream
3 Cadbury Creme Eggs, 2 chopped in pieces, 1 quartered (optional)

FOR THE FILLING

300g thick 0% fat Greek yoghurt
flesh of 3 passion fruit

You will need three 20cm sandwich tins.

1. Preheat the oven to 180°C/160°C fan/gas mark 4. Grease three 20cm sandwich tins and line the bases with non-stick baking parchment.

2. Beat together the butter and sugar in a large bowl with a hand-held mixer until the mixture is pale and creamy. Add the beaten egg a little at a time, beating well between each addition. Add the vanilla extract with the last of the egg.

3. Sift together the flour, bicarbonate of soda and cocoa, add half to the bowl and fold this in. Add the buttermilk, fold again then fold in the last of the flour mix. Add the cooled melted chocolate to the bowl and fold it in until everything is fully incorporated.

4. Divide the mixture between the three tins and bake the cakes in the oven for 30 minutes until they are browned and risen, and a skewer inserted in the middle comes out clean.

5. Leave the sponges to cool for 10 minutes in the tins before removing them and allowing them to cool completely on wire racks.

6. Meanwhile make the topping. Heat the cream in a small saucepan, add the Cadbury Creme Egg pieces and heat until the chocolate is melted and bubbling. Remove the pan from the heat and whisk until the mixture is smooth.

7. Make the filling by beating the yoghurt and folding the flesh of the three passion fruit into it.

8. Place one of the sponges on a serving plate, spread half the cream over it and put the second sponge on top. Spread the remaining cream over the second sponge and top with the third sponge. Pour the chocolate sauce over the top and gently spread it out into an even layer – take it right to the edges so that it drizzles down the sides.

9. Decorate the top with the quartered Cadbury Creme Egg pieces, if using. The cake can be kept in the fridge for a few hours, but take it out about 30 minutes before you want to eat it.

Per serving

384 kcals	19.5g fat	11g sat fat	26.5g sugar	0.3g salt

CADBURY CREME EGG PINATA CAKE

Cut open this cake and watch the Cadbury Mini Creme Eggs pour out in all their gooey glory. This is one surprise that's bound to start a party with a bang! This recipe is a very tasty but indulgent treat, best enjoyed on special occasions.

SERVES 18
PREP TIME 45 MINS,
PLUS COOLING
COOKING TIME 20–25 MINS

FOR THE SPONGE
200g unsalted butter, softened
275g caster sugar
3 medium eggs
1 tsp vanilla extract
275g self-raising flour
1 tsp baking powder
pinch of salt
6 tbsp skimmed milk

FOR THE GANACHE
225g dark chocolate, finely chopped
150g butter, cubed
1 tbsp golden syrup
220ml whipping cream
2 x 89g bags Cadbury Mini Creme Eggs

FOR THE ICING
100g icing sugar
orange food colouring
1 Cadbury Creme Egg

1. Preheat the oven to 180°C/160°C fan/gas mark 4. Grease three 18cm round tins and line the bases with baking parchment.

2. Cream together the butter and sugar in a large bowl with a hand-held whisk for 2–3 minutes until the mixture is light and fluffy. Beat in the eggs one at a time, then stir in the vanilla extract.

3. Add the flour, baking powder and salt, stir until the mixture is well combined, then add the milk. You should have a thick batter. Divide the mixture equally between the tins and smooth the tops with a spatula. Bake for 20–25 minutes, or until the sponges are risen and golden brown and a skewer comes out clean. Allow them to cool briefly in the tins, and then transfer them to a wire rack to cool completely.

4. To make the ganache, place the chocolate, butter and golden syrup in a large, heatproof bowl over a saucepan of boiling water, making sure that the bottom of the bowl does not touch the water. Stir until the mixture is melted and smooth and then pour in the cream and mix until combined. Put the ganache in the fridge for about 30 minutes, or until it is chilled but not set firm. Remove the bowl from the fridge and whip the ganache with an electric whisk until it turns from dark to pale brown; it should be light and mousse-like in texture.

5. To assemble the cake, stack the bottom two layers on top of each other. Use a circular 9cm cutter to remove the middle, pressing through both layers at once to make sure the holes line up. Put the bottom ring on a cake stand or plate and cover the top with a layer of ganache using a palette knife. Put the second ring on top of the first and fill the cavity with Cadbury Mini Creme Eggs. Make sure the hole is filled to the level of the top sponge so it doesn't cave in.

6. Cover the surface of the second sponge ring with ganache, then top with the third sponge. Cover the whole cake in the remaining ganache, using a palette knife to smooth the edges.

7. To make the icing, divide the icing sugar between two small bowls and add 1–2 teaspoons of water to each. You might need to add a little more water – you want a thick paste that you can drizzle. Add enough orange food colouring to one of the bowls to make a pale orange icing and drizzle them both over the cake. Pull apart the Cadbury Creme Egg and use it to decorate the top.

Per serving

453 kcals	26.8g fat	16.3g sat fat	35g sugar	0.2g salt

CADBURY CREME EGG DRIZZLE CAKE

Give this delicious drizzle cake a go and you won't look back. Guests will pour into your kitchen from the moment you take it out of the oven.

SERVES 12
PREP TIME 15–20 MINS
COOKING TIME 30–35 MINS

FOR THE SPONGE

60ml sunflower oil
160g caster sugar
1 egg
100g plain flour
35g cocoa powder
½ tsp bicarbonate of soda
½ tsp baking powder
¼ tsp salt
100ml milk

FOR THE ICING

100g icing sugar
orange food colouring
1 Cadbury Creme Egg

1. Preheat the oven to 180°C/160°C fan/gas mark 4 and grease and line a loaf tin with baking parchment.
2. Whisk together the oil, caster sugar and egg in a large bowl until the mixture is smooth and well combined.
3. In a separate bowl, sift together the flour, cocoa powder, bicarbonate of soda, baking powder and salt. Add half the dry ingredients to the wet mix and whisk to combine, and then add all the milk. Mix in the remaining dry ingredients and stir until the batter is smooth.
4. Pour the batter into the tin and bake in the oven for 30–35 minutes until the cake is risen and a skewer comes out clean. Leave the cake to cool briefly in the tin before transferring it to a wire rack to cool completely.
5. To make the icing, divide the icing sugar between two small bowls and add 1–2 teaspoons of water to each. You might need to add a little more water – you want a thick paste that you can drizzle. Add enough orange food colouring to one of the bowls to make a pale orange icing.
6. Drizzle the icing over the cool cake, allowing it to drip over the edges. Pull the Cadbury Creme Egg apart to allow the inside to seep out and arrange the pieces on top of the cake.

Per serving

176 kcals	6.6g fat	1.2g sat fat	16.5g sugar	0.2g salt

CADBURY CREME EGG TRAY BAKE

Bake up a gooey storm with this deliciously different treat in a tray. The light and fluffy bake combined with Cadbury Creme Egg-topped icing makes for a bake you can't beat!

SERVES 20
PREP TIME 20 MINS
COOKING TIME 25 MINS

175g butter, plus extra for greasing

175g caster sugar

3 eggs

150g self-raising flour, sifted

1 tsp baking powder

50g cocoa powder

100g icing sugar

3 Cadbury Creme Eggs, chopped into small pieces

1. Preheat the oven to 180°C/160°C fan/gas mark 4 and grease and line a shallow 30 x 20cm baking tin.
2. Beat together the butter and sugar in a bowl with a hand-held whisk until they are light and fluffy. Add the eggs one at a time, beating well after each addition. Add the flour, baking powder and 25g of the cocoa powder and fold them in.
3. Pour the mixture in the tin, pushing it into the corners and levelling the top.
4. Bake in oven for 20-25 minutes until a skewer pushed into the centre comes out clean.
5. Remove the tin from the oven, allow it to cool for 10 minutes, then remove from the tin and place it on a wire rack to cool completely.
6. Sift the icing sugar and remaining cocoa powder into a bowl and add 2 tablespoons of water to make a spreadable icing. Spread this over the top of the cooled cake and top with the pieces of Cadbury Creme Egg.

Per serving

192 kcals	9.4g fat	5.6g sat fat	17.7g sugar	0.07g salt

CADBURY CREME EGG, AMARETTI & RASPBERRY LAYERED POTS

This indulgent little dessert has it all. Crunchy amaretti biscuit?
Tick. Fresh raspberries? Tick. Smothered in Greek yoghurt and
a mouth-wateringly creamy Cadbury Creme Egg sauce? Tick, tick and tick!

SERVES 6
PREP TIME 15 MINS,
PLUS COOLING

50ml double cream
2 Cadbury Creme Eggs, chopped
into pieces, plus 1 extra to serve
(optional)
60g amaretti biscuits
300g 0% fat Greek yoghurt
150g raspberries

1. Pour the cream into a small, heavy-based saucepan and heat over a medium heat until it starts to simmer. Add two of the chopped Cadbury Creme Eggs and stir. Heat until the sauce begins to bubble and the Cadbury Creme Egg pieces have completely melted.
2. Remove from the heat and beat with a wooden spoon until smooth, then pour into a bowl to cool completely.
3. Break the amaretti biscuits into small pieces and divide them between six small glasses (about 100ml capacity). Pour a sixth of the Cadbury Creme Egg sauce into each one, then add a layer of Greek yoghurt.
4. Top with the raspberries and the remaining chopped Cadbury Creme Egg, if using, and serve. The pots will keep in the fridge for a couple of hours until you are ready to eat.

Per serving

174 kcals	7.2g fat	4g sat fat	20g sugar	0.4g salt

CADBURY CREME EGG
& BANANA PAVLOVA

Get a loada this Cadbury Creme Egg Pavlova. Banana brilliance topped with gorgeous gooey goodness. Eggstravagant? A bit. Delicious? You're damn right.

SERVES 10
PREP TIME 30 MINS
COOKING TIME 1 HOUR

3 egg whites
180g caster sugar
1 tsp cornflour
1 tsp white wine vinegar

FOR THE FILLING AND DRIZZLE
300ml whipping cream
2 Cadbury Creme Eggs, chopped
into pieces
1 banana

1. Preheat the oven to 120°C/100°C fan/gas mark ½. Line a large baking sheet with baking parchment.
2. Put the egg whites into a large, clean bowl and whisk with a hand-held whisk until they form stiff peaks. Add the sugar a spoonful at a time, whisking well between each addition and adding the cornflour and vinegar with the last spoonful of sugar. Whisk until the mixture is thick and glossy.
3. Spread the mixture into an egg shape about 20 x 25cm on the baking sheet, with higher sides and a dip in the middle. Create swirls on top of the sides with the back of a spoon.
4. Bake in the oven for 1 hour until crisp but not coloured. Turn off the oven, then leave the pavlova to cool in the oven for 1 hour. This prevents the meringue cracking as it cools.
5. Meanwhile make the drizzle. Heat 25ml of the cream in a small saucepan, add one of the chopped Cadbury Creme Eggs and heat until melted and bubbling slightly. Remove the pan from the heat and beat the mixture until it is smooth, then pour it into a bowl and leave it to cool completely.
6. Take the meringue out of the oven, peel off the baking parchment and place the meringue on a serving plate.
7. Pour the remaining cream into a bowl and whisk it with a hand-held whisk until soft peaks form. Pile it into the centre of the meringue. Slice the banana and arrange it on top of the cream with the remaining chopped Cadbury Creme Eggs. Finish by drizzling with the Cadbury Creme Egg sauce.

Per serving

234 kcals	12.8g fat	8g sat fat	25g sugar	0.3g salt

CADBURY CREME EGG & RASPBERRY TART

This not only looks good, it tastes unberrylievable. Give that traditional tart a Cadbury Creme Egg twist and we guarantee you won't regret it.

SERVES 12
PREP TIME 15 MINS
COOKING TIME 20 MINS

1 x 320g pack ready-rolled puff pastry

1 egg, lightly beaten

250g light soft cheese

250ml double cream

2 tbsp icing sugar

225g raspberries

4 Cadbury Creme Eggs, cut into quarters

10g milk chocolate

1. Preheat the oven to 200°C/180°C fan/gas mark 6 and line a large baking sheet with baking parchment.
2. Unroll the pastry and place it on the baking sheet. Use a small sharp knife to score a 1.5cm border around the edge and prick the pastry inside the border with a fork. This will ensure that the edge of the tart puffs up during cooking while the centre stays flat.
3. Brush the border with beaten egg and bake the pastry in the oven for 20 minutes until golden.
4. Remove the pastry from the oven and leave it to cool on a wire rack. If the middle of the tart puffs up during cooking press it down gently to flatten it before it cools completely.
5. Meanwhile beat together the soft cheese, cream and sugar until they are smooth. Once the pastry case is completely cold spread the mixture over the centre in an even layer.
6. Dot the raspberries over the cream filling, then put the Cadbury Creme Egg quarters between the raspberries. Finely grate the chocolate over the top and serve.

Per serving

337 kcals	23.2g fat	13.3g sat fat	13.5g sugar	0.4g salt

CADBURY CREME EGG BREAD & BUTTER PUDDING

With a Cadbury Creme Egg twist, this classic only gets butter!
Sweet and creamy, but eggceptionally light, this delicious pudding
will have everyone coming back for more.

SERVES 8
PREP TIME 15 MINS,
PLUS 1 HOUR RESTING
COOKING TIME 40 MINS

50g butter, softened

8 slices medium sliced white bread, crusts removed

2 Cadbury Creme Eggs, chopped into pieces

2 tbsp caster sugar

2 eggs

600ml semi-skimmed milk

1. Grease a rectangular ovenproof dish measuring 20 x 28 x 4cm with a little of the butter.
2. Butter the bread slices. Cut each slice into four triangles and lay half the pieces over the base of the dish, overlapping them slightly so they cover the base in a single layer.
3. Dot half the Cadbury Creme Egg pieces over the bread slices, then sprinkle over 1 tablespoon of the sugar. Repeat with the remaining bread, Cadbury Creme Egg pieces and sugar.
4. Lightly beat the eggs with the milk then pour the mixture into the dish, ensuring that you cover all the bread slices. Set aside for one hour to allow the bread to soften slightly.
5. Preheat the oven to 180°C/160°C fan/gas mark 4.
6. Bake the bread and butter pudding for 40 minutes until golden, then leave it to rest for 10 minutes before serving.

Per serving

250 kcals	10g fat	4.5g sat fat	14.5g sugar	0.5g salt

CADBURY CREME EGG FRANGIPANE TART

This tasty tart is a work of art thanks to the Cadbury Creme Eggstra special ingredient. Crack out this pastry and almond confection next time you're looking to impress.

SERVES 10
PREP TIME 15 MINS
COOKING TIME 25 MINS

75g butter, softened

75g golden caster sugar

1 egg, lightly beaten (set 1 tsp aside to brush pastry edges)

75g ground almonds

2 tbsp plain flour

1 x 375g pack ready-rolled shortcrust pastry

225g raspberries

2 Cadbury Creme Eggs, each cut into 8 pieces

1. Preheat the oven to 200°C/180°C fan/gas mark 6 and line a large baking sheet with baking parchment.
2. Cream together the butter and sugar until the mixture is pale and fluffy, then beat in the egg followed by the ground almonds and the flour. Mix until they are combined and you have a smooth frangipane paste.
3. Unroll the pastry sheet and trim off the corners to create an oval shape, then lay it on the baking sheet. Spread the frangipane in an even layer over the pastry, leaving a 2.5cm border around the edge.
4. Arrange the raspberries over the frangipane. Fold the pastry border over the edge of the filling to create an edge to the tart and brush this with the reserved beaten egg.
5. Bake the tart in the oven for 20 minutes, then take it out and dot the Cadbury Creme Egg pieces among the fruit. Return to the oven and bake for a further 5 minutes until the pastry is golden and the Cadbury Creme Eggs have just begun to melt. Serve warm or cold.

Per serving

374 kcals	23.8g fat	9.8g sat fat	14.5g sugar	0.2g salt

 TIP Replace the raspberries with pears: peel and core 2 pears, cut each one into eight slices, arrange them over the frangipane and bake as above.

CADBURY CREME EGG ICE-CREAM SANDWICHES

Who said sandwiches have to be savoury? These sweet summertime snacks make the perfect frozen treat!

SERVES 4
PREP TIME 15 MINS, PLUS COOLING AND FREEZING

50ml whipping cream
2 Cadbury Creme Eggs, chopped into pieces
8 rectangular ice-cream wafers
4 x 40g slices vanilla ice-cream cut from a block

1. Pour the cream into a small, heavy-based saucepan and heat over a medium heat until it starts to simmer. Add the Cadbury Creme Egg pieces and stir. Heat until the sauce begins to bubble and the Cadbury Creme Egg pieces have completely melted.

2. Remove the pan from the heat and beat the mixture with a wooden spoon until it is smooth, then pour it into a bowl to cool completely.

3. Spread one side of each wafer with a little of the sauce until it is covered, then chill the wafers in the fridge for 30 minutes to set.

4. Put a slice of ice-cream between the coated sides of two wafers to create a sandwich, then repeat with the other three slices of ice-cream.

5. Dip the ends of each sandwich in the remaining Cadbury Creme Egg sauce, then place them on a small baking sheet lined with baking parchment and freeze them for 30 minutes.

6. Serve or wrap each ice-cream sandwich individually in baking parchment and store them in the freezer for 2–3 weeks.

Per serving

185 kcals	10g fat	6g sat fat	16g sugar	0.2g salt

CADBURY CREME EGG & ORANGE RICE PUDDING

If you're looking for a lighter treat that's rice and easy, this gooey take on an old school classic is the one for you. Cadbury Creme Egg comfort food at its absolute finest.

SERVES 8
PREP TIME 10 MINS
COOKING TIME 25 MINS

200g short-grain pudding rice

25g butter

30g golden caster sugar

800ml skimmed milk

finely grated zest of 1 orange

2 Cadbury Creme Eggs, roughly chopped

1. Put all the ingredients except the Cadbury Creme Eggs in a large saucepan and bring the mixture to the boil. Simmer gently for 20–25 minutes, stirring occasionally, until the rice grains are tender but still have a slight bite.
2. Remove the pan from the heat and leave the mixture to cool for 10–15 minutes, stirring it every now and then to prevent a skin forming.
3. Lightly mix the Cadbury Creme Egg pieces into the rice pudding until they start to melt, then swirl them through the pudding.
4. Divide the rice pudding between small bowls or glasses to serve. You can also serve it cold.

Per serving

208 kcals	5g fat	2.8g sat fat	15g sugar	0.1g salt

CADBURY CREME EGG
QUEEN OF PUDDINGS

Don't be throne off by the prep time. This is one of the crown jewels of British baking. An epic collision of custard, cake and Cadbury Creme Egg fit for a queen.

SERVES 8
PREP TIME 30 MINS,
PLUS 30 MINS SOAKING
COOKING TIME 45–50 MINS

FOR THE BASE
75g fresh white breadcrumbs
600ml skimmed milk
50g caster sugar
3 egg yolks
1 tsp vanilla bean paste

FOR THE CADBURY CREME EGG LAYER
75ml whipping cream
3 Cadbury Creme Eggs, chopped into pieces

FOR THE MERINGUE TOPPING
3 egg whites
180g caster sugar

Per serving

292 kcals	6.8g fat	3.8g sat fat	41.3g sugar	0.2g salt

1. Butter a 15 x 25cm ovenproof dish and add the breadcrumbs.
2. In a small pan gently heat the milk and sugar, stirring until the sugar has dissolved.
3. Put the egg yolks and vanilla in a bowl and lightly whisk together, then whisk in the milk. Pour this custard over the breadcrumbs and leave them to soak for 30 minutes. Preheat the oven to 170°C/150°C fan/gas mark 3.
4. Put the dish inside a roasting tin and fill the tin with boiling water to halfway up the sides of the dish. Bake the pudding for 30 minutes until it is golden and set, then remove the dish from the roasting tin and leave it to cool.
5. Meanwhile make the Cadbury Creme Egg layer. Put the cream in a small saucepan and heat it over a medium heat until it starts to simmer. Add the Cadbury Creme Egg pieces and heat until the mixture begins to bubble, stirring until the chocolate has melted. Remove the pan from the heat and beat the mixture with a wooden spoon until it is smooth, then pour it into a bowl to cool slightly.
6. To make the meringue, put the egg whites in a large bowl and whisk them with an electric whisk to stiff peaks. Add the sugar a spoonful at a time, whisking well after each addition.
7. Pour the Cadbury Creme Egg sauce over the custard, then spoon the meringue on top and swirl the top slightly. Bake for 15–20 minutes until the meringue is crisp and golden. Serve hot or cold.

CADBURY CREME EGG CHOCOLATE POTS

These little bad boys really hit the spot. Thanks to the eggstra special ingredient, these rich and gooey delights will drive your guests potty.

SERVES 6
PREP TIME 20 MINS,
PLUS 4 HOURS CHILLING

100ml double cream
5 Cadbury Creme Eggs, 4 chopped into small pieces and 1 chopped into 6 pieces
3 tbsp cocoa
3 egg whites

1. Heat the cream, four of the Cadbury Creme Eggs and the cocoa in a heavy-based pan until the Cadbury Creme Eggs melt and the mixture starts to bubble.
2. Remove the pan from the heat and whisk the mixture until smooth, then leave it to cool for 10 minutes.
3. Whisk the egg whites until they are stiff, stir in a large spoonful of the cooled Cadbury Creme Egg mixture to loosen them slightly then gently fold in the rest. Try to mix as gently as possible to keep the mixture light and airy.
4. Divide the mixture between six small glasses or ramekins (about 125ml each) and chill for at least 4 hours.
5. Top each chocolate pot with a piece of the last Cadbury Creme Egg and serve immediately.

Per serving

192 kcals	10.8g fat	8g sat fat	16.5g sugar	0.1g salt

CADBURY CREME EGG ICE-CREAM

Yes you could just buy ice-cream from the shop. But where's the fun (and the Creme Egg) in that? Plus you get to say you made your own ice-cream, so it's a win-win!

SERVES 12
PREP TIME 20 MINS,
PLUS COOLING AND
FREEZING

400ml full-fat milk
400ml double cream
1 vanilla pod
6 egg yolks
150g caster sugar
4 Cadbury Creme Eggs, chopped into small pieces

1. Put the milk and cream in a large pan, then split the vanilla pod lengthways and scrape the seeds into the pan along with the halves of the pod. Heat over a medium heat until just simmering. Remove the pan from the heat and leave it to cool for 15 minutes.

2. Whisk together the egg yolks and sugar in a large bowl until they are thick and creamy. Slowly add the milk and cream, whisking all the time.

3. Return the mixture to the pan then cook over a gentle heat for 10–15 minutes. Stir continuously until the custard coats the back of the spoon – when you draw your finger across the spoon it should leave a path through the custard.

4. Remove the pan from the heat, pour the mixture back into the bowl, cover the surface with cling film to prevent a skin forming and leave it to cool completely.

5. Once the custard is cold remove the vanilla pod halves then pour it into a large lidded plastic box. Put the lid on and freeze for an hour until the ice-cream starts to freeze around the edges, then remove it from the freezer and beat it with a wooden spoon. Freeze it again for another hour.

6. Remove the ice-cream again and beat it until it is smooth, then fold in the chopped Cadbury Creme Eggs and freeze again for another hour. Beat once more, then leave it to freeze for another 3–4 hours, or ideally overnight, until completely frozen.

7. Remove the ice-cream from the freezer for 15 minutes to allow it to soften slightly before scooping.

Per serving

311 kcals	22g fat	13.2g sat fat	23.4g sugar	0.09g salt

CADBURY CREME EGG PROFITEROLES

Perfect these profiteroles and you'll have everyone eating out of the palm of your hand. This sweet and savoury speggtacle is a showstopper of epic proportions.

SERVES 8 (MAKES 24 PROFITEROLES)
PREP TIME 45 MINS
COOKING TIME 25 MINS

FOR THE PROFITEROLES
75g butter
1 tsp caster sugar
50g plain flour
50g strong white flour
3 eggs, lightly beaten

FOR THE FILLING
200ml whipping cream
2 Cadbury Creme Eggs, chopped
100g light soft cheese

FOR THE CHOCOLATE SAUCE
110g plain dark chocolate
1 Cadbury Creme Egg, chopped
75ml water

You will need a piping bag and nozzles

1. Preheat the oven to 200°C/180°C fan/gas mark 6 and line two baking sheets with baking parchment.
2. To make the profiteroles put the butter and sugar in a saucepan with 175ml water and heat gently until the butter has melted. Bring the mixture to a rolling boil then remove the pan from the heat add both flours and beat until smooth.
3. Return the pan to the heat and cook for 1–2 minutes, stirring continuously until the paste starts to come away from the sides of the pan. Spoon the mixture into a large bowl and leave it to cool for a few minutes.
4. Add the beaten eggs to the paste a little at a time, beating well between each addition. The dough should be glossy and smooth with a soft dropping consistency – you might not need to add all the egg.
5. Spoon the dough into a large piping bag fitted with a 1cm plain nozzle and pipe walnut-sized rounds on to the baking sheets, leaving a 2cm gap between each one.
6. Bake the profiteroles in the oven for 20–25 minutes until they are golden and crisp. Remove the profiteroles from the oven and leave them to cool slightly on the baking sheets, then cut a small slit in the side of each one and put them on a wire rack to cool completely.

Per serving

388 kcals	28g fat	16.8g sat fat	22g sugar	1.9g salt

7. Meanwhile make the filling. Heat 50ml of the cream in a small pan, add the Cadbury Creme Egg pieces and heat until they have melted and the mixture is bubbling. Remove the pan from the heat and whisk until the mixture is smooth, then pour it into a bowl to cool.

8. Once cool beat the soft cheese into the mixture and put the bowl in the fridge for an hour to allow it to thicken slightly. Whip the remaining cream until soft peaks start to form, then whisk in the cooled soft cheese mixture until it is fully incorporated.

9. Spoon the filling into a piping bag fitted with a 1cm plain nozzle then fill each profiterole by piping the cream through the slit.

10. To make the chocolate sauce, put the chocolate. chopped Cadbury Creme Egg and water in a heatproof bowl suspended over a pan of gently simmering water. Stir until the chocolate melts and you have a smooth sauce.

11. Serve the profiteroles in bowls with the sauce poured over the top.

CADBURY CREME EGG & AVOCADO MOUSSE

Spruce up your mousse with Cadbury Creme Eggs and avocado.
Yes, we know it sounds weird but trust us, it tastes amazing!

SERVES 6
PREP TIME 15 MINS, PLUS COOLING AND CHILLING

2 tbsp runny honey

4 Cadbury Creme Eggs, chopped into pieces

50ml skimmed milk

2 ripe avocados, stoned and peeled

4 tbsp cocoa powder

1. Put the honey, Cadbury Creme Egg pieces and milk in a small saucepan, and heat them gently until the mixture is bubbling, stirring continuously. Remove the pan from the heat, whisk the mixture until it is smooth then leave it to cool completely.

2. Whizz the avocado flesh In a food processor until it is smooth. Add the Cadbury Creme Egg mixture and the cocoa powder and whizz again until the mixture is completely smooth and glossy. You will need to scrape the mix from the sides to ensure that everything is incorporated.

3. Divide the mousse between six small ramekins and chill until you are ready to serve.

Per serving

220 kcals	10g fat	4.5g sat fat	22g sugar	0.15g salt

CADBURY CREME EGG BAKED ALASKA

Break the mould with this mouth-watering version of baked Alaska.
When meringue, sponge and Cadbury Creme Egg collide, the result
is always incredible.

SERVES 12
PREP TIME 45 MINS
COOKING TIME 20 MINS

FOR THE SPONGE
2 eggs
60g caster sugar
60g plain flour

FOR THE FILLING AND SAUCE
1 litre vanilla ice-cream
4 Cadbury Creme Eggs, cut
into pieces
50ml double cream

FOR THE MERINGUE
3 egg whites
180g caster sugar

You will need a 15cm-diameter
pudding basin

1. Preheat the oven to 200°C/180°C fan/gas mark 6. Grease a
   20cm sandwich tin and line the base with baking parchment.
2. For the sponge, put the eggs and sugar in a large bowl and
   whisk them for about 5 minutes with a hand-held mixer,
   until the mixture becomes very pale and thick and leaves
   a ribbon-like trail when you lift the mixer from the bowl.
   Gently fold the flour into the mixture, then spoon it into the
   tin and bake it in the oven until it is golden and starting to
   shrink away from the edges, about 10 minutes.
3. Remove the tin from the oven and leave the sponge to cool
   for 5 minutes in the tin, then take it out of the tin and allow
   it to cool completely on a wire rack.
4. Take the ice-cream out of the freezer and leave it to soften
   for about 15 minutes. Grease the pudding basin and line it
   with cling film. Stir half the Cadbury Creme Egg pieces into
   the softened ice-cream, then spoon it into the basin and
   freeze it for a couple of hours until it is solid.
5. To make the chocolate sauce, heat the cream and the rest
   of the Cadbury Creme Egg pieces in a small pan until the
   chocolate starts to melt and the mixture begins to bubble.
   Remove the pan from the heat and whisk the mixture until it
   is smooth. Pour it into a bowl and leave it to cool.

Per serving

273 kcals	8g fat	5.6g sat fat	39g sugar	0.1g salt

6. Preheat the oven to 200°C/fan 180°C/gas mark 6. Put the sponge on a flat ovenproof serving plate and spread the chocolate sauce on top. Move the ice-cream from the freezer to the fridge and leave it to soften for 10 minutes while you make the meringue.

7. Whisk the egg whites in a large bowl with a hand-held whisk until they are stiff, then add the sugar a spoonful at a time, whisking well between each addition, until the meringue is thick and glossy. Turn the ice-cream on to the sponge then spoon the meringue on top, making sure that you cover the ice-cream and sponge completely in a thick even layer. Lightly swirl a pattern in the meringue with the back of a spoon, then bake it in the oven for 8–10 minutes until golden. Serve immediately.

CADBURY CREME EGG COCONUT & MANGO PARFAIT

Oeuf la la! This delightful dessert certainly has the eggs factor. Perfect for impressing special guests while keeping your cool.

SERVES 14
PREP TIME 30 MINS,
PLUS FREEZING

2 x 500g tubs coconut ice-cream
1 x 500g tub mango sorbet
100ml single cream
4 Cadbury Creme Eggs, chopped into pieces

Per serving

229 kcals	9g fat	7g sat fat	25.7g sugar	1.1g salt

1. Grease and line a 900g loaf tin with a double layer of cling film, leaving some overhanging the edges so you can pull the parfait out of the tin once frozen.

2. Remove one tub of coconut ice-cream from the freezer and leave it to soften for about 15 minutes. Turn the ice-cream into a bowl and beat it for a few minutes until it has softened further, then spread it in an even layer over the base of the loaf tin and return the tin to the freezer for an hour.

3. Repeat the softening and beating with the mango sorbet. Spread this in a layer on top of the coconut ice-cream, then return the tin to the freezer for another hour.

4. Add a final layer of coconut ice-cream using the same method, then put the loaf tin back in the freezer for 2–3 hours to freeze again fully.

5. Make the chocolate coating by heating the cream and the chopped Cadbury Creme Eggs in a small pan until the chocolate starts to melt and the mixture begins to bubble. Remove the pan from the heat, whisk the mixture until it is smooth and pour it into a bowl. Leave it to cool.

6. Take the loaf tin out of the freezer and dip it in a bowl of warm water to release the parfait from the tin. Turn it out on to a serving plate and remove the cling film. Pour the coating over the top and gently spread it down the sides to coat the ice-cream completely.

7. Leave the parfait for 10 minutes to allow the coating to set and the ice-cream to soften enough to slice, then cut it into slices to serve.

CADBURY CREME EGG WITH PINEAPPLE FRITTERS

These Cadbury Creme Egg fritters are eggsceptional. Sweet, creamy and with just the right amount of tang – as soon as these bundles of deliciousness are gone, you'll be pining for more!

SERVES 8
PREP TIME 15 MINS
COOKING TIME 10 MINS

FOR THE CADBURY CREME EGG SAUCE

50ml whipping cream
2 Cadbury Creme Eggs, chopped into pieces

FOR THE FRITTERS

1 litre vegetable oil, for frying
200g self-raising flour
225ml sparkling elderflower water, chilled
1 medium pineapple, peeled, cored and cut into 8 slices
2 Cadbury Creme Eggs, quartered, to serve (optional)

1. To make the sauce heat the cream in a small pan, add the chopped Cadbury Creme Eggs and heat until the chocolate has melted and the mixture is bubbling. Remove the pan from the heat and whisk until the mixture is smooth.
2. Heat the oil in a large, deep frying pan until it is at 180°C. If you don't have a thermometer the oil will be at the right temperature when a small piece of bread dropped into it turns golden in 1 minute.
3. While the oil is heating make the fritter batter. Put the flour in a large bowl and whisk in the elderflower water until the batter is thick enough to coat the pineapple slices.
4. Cook four pineapple slices at a time. First dip them in the batter, then gently lower them into the hot oil one at a time. Cook them for 4 minutes until they are golden, carefully turning them over halfway through cooking. Remove the slices from the oil with a slotted spoon and place them on a plate covered in kitchen paper. Put the plate in a warm place while you cook the remaining four slices.
5. Serve each fritter with a Cadbury Creme Egg quarter in the centre, if using, and the sauce drizzled over the top.

Per serving

208 kcals	7.8g fat	2.7g sat fat	11.8g sugar	0.2g salt

CADBURY CREME EGG CHOCOLATE FONDANTS

These fondants will really impress your guests; each one has a gooey surprise hidden in the centre! But remember that they are fragile and need to be flipped with care.

MAKES 8
PREP TIME 45 MINS
COOKING TIME 10–12 MINS

125g unsalted butter, plus extra for brushing

cocoa powder, for dusting

125g dark chocolate, broken into pieces

3 medium eggs

125g caster sugar

40g plain flour, sifted

8 Cadbury Mini Creme Eggs

1. Preheat the oven to 180°C/160°fan/gas mark 4.
2. Prepare eight ramekins or fondant moulds by brushing the insides with melted butter and then adding a thin even dusting of cocoa powder.
3. Put a heatproof bowl over a small pan of simmering water and melt the chocolate and butter together until they are smooth. Mix to combine.
4. In a separate bowl, whisk the eggs with a hand-held whisk until they increase in volume then gradually add the sugar. Once all the sugar is added, keep whisking until the mixture is thickened, pale and fluffy.
5. Pour the melted chocolate and butter into the egg mixture and fold them through. Add the flour and fold that in too.
6. Pour the mixture into the ramekins or moulds, only filling them half full. Place a Cadbury Mini Creme Egg on top of the mixture in each ramekin and then cover it with the remaining mixture.
7. Bake the fondants in the oven for 10–12 minutes until cracks start to appear around the outside and the centre is still soft.
8. Remove the fondants from the oven and carefully flip them on to a large serving plate. Serve them with ice-cream or whipped cream and watch the Cadbury Creme Egg ooze out!

Per serving

352 kcals	21g fat	12.3g sat fat	31.5g sugar	0.1g salt

FANCY CADBURY CREME EGG CHEESECAKE

For a great way to entertain your guests, look no further than this deliciously decadent sweet treat. When you mix Cadbury Creme Eggs into a cheesecake the result is astonishing!

SERVES 16
PREP TIME 1 HOUR, PLUS CHILLING

150g digestive biscuits, crushed into fine crumbs

75g butter, melted

750g light soft cheese

seeds from 1 vanilla pod

150g icing sugar, sifted

300ml double cream

8 Cadbury Mini Creme Eggs, halved

TO DECORATE

30g white chocolate, melted

30g dark chocolate, melted

8 Cadbury Mini Creme Eggs (optional)

You will need a 20cm cake ring or spring form tin

1. Line the inside of the tin or ring with some acetate to make it easier to remove the cheesecake once it has set.
2. Put the biscuit crumbs in a bowl and stir in the melted butter. Pack the mixture into the cake tin and press it down into the bottom of the tin so the whole surface is covered. Put the tin in the fridge to set.
3. In a bowl, beat together the cream cheese, the vanilla seeds and sifted icing sugar with a hand-held whisk. In a separate bowl, whisk the double cream until it starts to firm up. Gently fold the cream into the cream cheese and mix until combined.
4. Remove the biscuit case from the fridge and arrange the eight halved Cadbury Mini Creme Eggs on top lengthways and facing out around the sides of the tin (use the goo to make them stick to the sides). Spoon in the cheese mixture and flatten the top with a spatula or palette knife.
5. Return the tin to the fridge for at least 1 hour.
6. Once set, take the cheesecake out of the fridge and remove the tin and acetate, being careful not to damage the outside of the cake.
7. Drizzle over the melted white and dark chocolate in a criss-cross pattern. If decorating, crush or halve the Cadbury Mini Creme Eggs and arange around the outside of the cheesecake and serve.

Per serving

321 kcals	22.6g fat	14g sat fat	19.3g sugar	0.5g salt

CADBURY CREME EGG GOOEY BISCUIT POSSET POTS

Try these lovely little biscuit pots for a chocolatey treat. You'll fall head over heels for their heart-shaped biscuits and ganache kisses.

SERVES 10
PREP TIME 1 HOUR
COOKING TIME 1 HOUR

FOR THE POSSET
450ml single cream
150g golden caster sugar
zest and juice of 1 orange
and ½ lemon
2 Cadbury Creme Eggs,
chopped into pieces

FOR THE CHOCOLATE BISCUITS
60g unsalted butter
30g golden caster sugar
few drops vanilla extract
1 small egg yolk
75g plain flour
¼ tsp fine sea salt
zest of 1 orange
40g milk chocolate chips

Per serving

371 kcals	20.7g fat	12.8g sat fat	34g sugar	0.22g salt

1. To make the posset, put the cream, sugar and citrus zest in a saucepan and bring them to a gentle simmer. Turn up the heat and bubble the mixture for 4–5 minutes, then stir in the juice. Strain the mixture into a jug and allow it to cool for 10–15 minutes.

2. Mix the Cadbury Creme Egg pieces into the posset mixture and stir until they are well distributed. Divide the mixture between ten ramekins.

3. To make the biscuit dough mix the butter and sugar in a large bowl with a wooden spoon or a hand-held mixer, then add the vanilla extract and the egg yolk and beat the mixture to combine everything. Sift over the flour and salt then add the orange zest and the milk chocolate chips. Slowly mix everything together – you might have to bring the dough together with your hands.

4. Preheat the oven to 180°C/160°C fan/gas mark 4. Flatten the dough into a thick pancake shape, wrap it in cling film and put it in the fridge for 10–15 minutes. Line a baking tray with baking parchment.

5. Roll out the chilled dough to the thickness of £1 coin on a lightly floured surface, then cut out small heart shapes. Place the biscuits on the baking tray and bake them for 11–15 minutes. Remove the tray from the oven and put the biscuits on a wire rack.

FOR THE GANACHE KISSES

40g milk chocolate and 40g dark chocolate, chopped into small pieces

1 Cadbury Creme Egg, chopped into pieces

50ml single cream

TO DECORATE (OPTIONAL)

insides of 2 Cadbury Creme Eggs

You will need a piping bag and nozzle

6. To make the ganache put the milk and dark chocolate and the Cadbury Creme Egg pieces in a bowl. Heat the cream in a small saucepan and bring it just to the boil. Pour the cream over the chocolate and leave it to sit for a minute, then stir until the mixture is smooth. Allow the ganache to cool, then put it in the fridge until you are ready to use it.

7. To make the ganache kisses whip the chilled mixture until it is smooth and light. Put the ganache in a piping bag with a nozzle, then pipe a few kisses on top of each posset. Add a chocolate heart biscuit for every ganache kiss. Then if adding extra decoration scoop out the insides of the Cadbury Creme Eggs and drizzle them over the top of the ramekins.

CADBURY CREME EGG PANCAKE CALZONE

Here's a recipe you can't refuse! A goo-infused pancake folded into a thick semicircle to resemble the godfather of all baked goods: the calzone!

MAKES 8
PREP TIME 20 MINS
COOKING TIME 30 MINS

FOR THE PANCAKES
100g plain flour
¼ tsp fine sea salt
1 tbsp caster sugar
2 large eggs
300ml skimmed milk
¼ tsp vanilla extract
insides of 2 Cadbury Creme Eggs
2 knobs butter, melted
vegetable oil, for frying

FOR THE FILLING
100g dark chocolate, broken into small pieces
2 Cadbury Creme Eggs, chopped into pieces

1. For the pancake mix, sift the flour, salt and caster sugar into a large bowl and begin to mix them together with a whisk, then make a little well in the centre. Put the eggs into the well and mix until everything is well combined.

2. Add the milk, pouring it in a thin stream and stirring continuously, then add the vanilla extract and the insides of 2 Cadbury Creme Eggs.

3. For the filling, melt the chopped Cadbury Creme Egg pieces and the dark chocolate in a microwave or in a heatproof bowl placed over a saucepan of water heated to a gentle simmer (do not allow the bottom of the bowl to touch the water).

4. To make the sauce, melt the chocolate in a heatproof bowl placed over a saucepan of simmering water as described above, stirring occasionally until it is completely melted. Stir the rest of the ingredients into the melted chocolate until the mixture is smooth. Remove the saucepan from the heat and put to one side to cool.

5. Now it's time to fry the pancakes. Mix the melted butter and vegetable oil in a small bowl. You will use this to grease the frying pan between each pancake. Heat the pan over a medium heat, then brush it with the buttery mixture. Pour a ladle of mixture into the frying pan, then take the pan off the heat and tilt it until the mixture covers the base.

CONTINUED OVERLEAF...

FOR THE SAUCE

50g dark chocolate, broken into small pieces

1 Cadbury Creme Eggs, chopped into pieces

25g butter

125ml single cream

1 tbsp caster sugar

few drops vanilla extract

TO DECORATE (OPTIONAL)

Cadbury Creme Eggs, melted (optional)

icing sugar, for dusting

6. Return the pan to the heat and wait for the pancake to cook – this shouldn't take longer than a minute, so watch it carefully. To check whether the pancake is ready, gently lift an edge for a sneak peek – if it's golden brown underneath it is ready.

7. Pour a generous splatter of the filling on to the pancake. Then lift one edge and gently fold the pancake in half, forming a semicircle in the pan. Allow the folded pancake to cook for a couple more minutes before removing and placing it on a plate. Repeat the process until all the mixture is used up.

8. Once all the pancakes are cooked, put them on a large tray or plate and decorate them with a little more melted Cadbury Creme Egg, if using, and squiggles of the sauce. Then dust them with icing sugar and serve.

Per serving

377 kcals	19.5g fat	10g sat fat	31.8g sugar	0.3g salt

CADBURY CREME EGG
SMASHED ICE-CREAM DESSERT

These topsy-turvy treats are perfect for the summer months. Help your guests cool off with an upside-down ice-cream with delectable Cadbury Creme Egg topping.

SERVES 4
PREP TIME 15 MINS

50ml whipping cream
2 Cadbury Creme Eggs, chopped
4 ice-cream cones
4 scoops strawberry ice-cream
2 tbsp roasted chopped hazelnuts

1. Put the cream in a small, heavy-based saucepan and heat it over a medium heat until it starts to simmer. Add half the Cadbury Creme Egg pieces and stir until they are melted. Continue heating until the sauce begins to bubble.
2. Remove the pan from the heat and beat the mixture with a wooden spoon until it is smooth, then leave it to cool slightly.
3. Dip the tip of each ice-cream cone in the Cadbury Creme Egg sauce. Place a scoop of ice-cream on four plates, then put one cone upside down on each plate on top of the ice-cream. Drizzle the sauce over the ice-cream then scatter over the hazelnuts and the rest of the Cadbury Creme Egg pieces and serve immediately.

Per serving

228 kcals	12g fat	6g sat fat	21g sugar	0.12g salt

TIP Replace the strawberry ice-cream with Cadbury Creme Egg Ice-cream (see recipe page 71) to fully embrace the Cadbury Creme Egg!

CADBURY CREME EGG MINI STICKY DATE PUDDINGS

There's no danger of over-egging the pudding with this tasty twist on a timeless treat. The gooey Cadbury Creme Egg custard contrasts with the heat of the sponge, so the proof is in the pudding! This recipe is a very tasty but indulgent treat, best enjoyed on special occasions.

SERVES 10
PREP TIME 35 MINS
COOKING TIME 1 HOUR

FOR THE SPONGE

225g Medjool dates, stoned and chopped into pieces

1 tsp vanilla extract

175g self-raising flour, plus extra for dusting

1 tsp bicarbonate of soda

70g demerara sugar

70g soft dark brown sugar

85g unsalted butter

2 eggs, lightly beaten

1 tbsp black treacle

1 tbsp golden syrup

100ml skimmed milk

10 Cadbury Mini Creme Eggs

1. Put the chopped dates in a bowl and pour 175ml boiling water over them. Leave them for 30 minutes, then mash them with a fork and add the vanilla extract.

2. Grease the mini pudding moulds and dust them with flour. Preheat the oven to 180°C/160°C fan/gas mark 4.

3. To make the puddings mix together the flour and bicarbonate of soda in a bowl. Beat both sugars and the butter together in a separate large bowl until creamy. Add the beaten egg a little at a time, beating well between additions. Beat in the black treacle and golden syrup. Use a large spoon to gently fold in some of the flour mixture, then half the milk, followed by the rest of the milk and flour, until everything is well combined. Finally, stir in the mashed dates.

4. Divide the mixture between the pudding moulds, then put one Cadbury Mini Creme Egg in each mould. Put the moulds on a baking tray and bake them for 20–25 minutes until well risen.

5. While the puddings are baking make the custard. Put the cream, milk, vanilla bean paste, grated nutmeg and the Cadbury Creme Egg insides into a saucepan and bring them to a gentle boil. Put the sugar and cornflour in a large bowl with the egg yolks and whisk until the mixture is smooth.

FOR THE CUSTARD

100ml single cream

350ml skimmed milk

1 tsp vanilla bean paste

¼ nutmeg, grated

insides of 2 Cadbury Creme Eggs

100g caster sugar

1½ tbsp cornflour

2 large egg yolks

TO DECORATE (OPTIONAL)

12 Cadbury Mini Creme Eggs

You will need 10 mini pudding moulds

6. When the milk mixture boils, pour it over the egg mixture in a thin steady stream, stirring continuously. Pour the mixture back into the saucepan and cook over a low heat, stirring continuously until the custard is thick enough to coat the back of a spoon. Pour the custard into a jug, then place cling film over the surface to prevent a skin forming.

7. Carefully remove the puddings from the moulds and place them on a wire rack.

8. Serve the puddings in shallow bowls with custard poured around them. Thinly slice the Cadbury Mini Creme Eggs for decoration, if using, and scatter the slices over the top of the puddings.

Per serving

447 kcals	14.4g fat	8.2g sat fat	53.4g sugar	0.4g salt

CADBURY CREME EGG & STRAWBERRY CRUMPETS

You'll struggle to beat these cracking Cadbury Creme Egg crumpets! They're sweet, savoury and super-simple to make.

SERVES 6
PREP TIME 15 MINS,
PLUS COOLING

50ml whipping cream
2 Cadbury Creme Eggs, chopped into pieces, plus extra to serve (optional)
50g light soft cheese
6 crumpets
300g strawberries, hulled and halved or quartered

1. Pour the cream into a small, heavy-based saucepan and heat over a medium heat until it starts to simmer. Add the chopped Cadbury Creme Eggs and stir. Continue to heat until the sauce begins to bubble and the Cadbury Creme Eggs have completely melted.

2. Remove the pan from the heat and beat the mixture with a wooden spoon until it is smooth, then pour it into a bowl to cool.

3. Once the mixture is cool add the soft cheese and mix until smooth with a hand whisk.

4. Lightly toast the crumpets then spread a spoonful of the Cadbury Creme Egg sauce on each one. Top with strawberry pieces and drizzle the remaining sauce on top. Serve immediately.

5. The sauce will keep in a jam jar or sealed container in the fridge for up to a week.

Per serving

223 kcals	7g fat	3.8g sat fat	14.5g sugar	0.5g sal

CADBURY CREME EGG FROZEN BERRIES

This is the perfect pick-me-up. Made in minutes – and, needless to say, it tastes berry, berry good!

SERVES 6
PREP TIME 10 MINS

600g frozen summer fruits
100ml single cream
2 Cadbury Creme Eggs,
chopped into pieces

1. Divide the fruit between six shallow bowls and leave it for 10 minutes to defrost slightly.
2. Meanwhile heat the cream in a small saucepan until it is just boiling and add the chopped Cadbury Creme Eggs. Stir until they are melted and the mixture is bubbling slightly.
3. Remove the pan from the heat, pour the hot sauce over the fruit and serve immediately.

Per serving

122 kcals	5.4g fat	3g sat fat	13.4g sugar	0.05g salt

CADBURY CREME EGG FUDGE

With its soft chocolate centre covered in rich Cadbury Creme Egg chaos, we'll let you be the judge of our delicious fudge.

MAKES 60 SQUARES
PREP TIME 15 MINS
COOKING TIME 25 MINS,
PLUS COOLING (6 HOURS)

300g caster sugar

300ml double cream

100g butter

75g dark chocolate, chopped into small pieces

1 tsp vanilla extract

3 Cadbury Creme Eggs, chopped into pieces

You will need a sugar thermometer

1. Line a 16 x 24cm shallow baking tin with baking parchment.
2. Put the sugar, cream and butter into a large saucepan and heat them gently, stirring, until the sugar is dissolved. Make sure you don't leave any sugar crystals on the sides of the pan as this will affect the texture of the fudge. Brush them down with a pastry brush if necessary.
3. Turn up the heat and boil the mixture for 10–15 minutes, stirring regularly to ensure that it doesn't burn on the bottom of the pan, until it reaches 115°C on a sugar thermometer.
4. Remove the pan from the heat and add the chocolate pieces and the vanilla extract. Beat the mixture well with a wooden spoon for 5–10 minutes until the fudge thickens and loses its shine.
5. Pour the fudge into the baking tin, smooth the surface with the back of a spoon and leave it to cool for about 15 minutes. Lightly press the Cadbury Creme Egg pieces into the top of the fudge, then leave it to cool completely. Cut into 2.5cm squares.

Per serving

73 kcals	4.5g fat	2.8g sat fat	7g sugar	0.01g salt

CADBURY CREME EGG PUFF PASTRY TWISTS

Puffect these puff pastries and you're on to a winner. Light and fluffy with a gorgeous gooey centre, these make a delicious dessert that will last for seconds.

MAKES 16
PREP TIME 15 MINS
COOKING TIME 15 MINS

1 x 320g pack ready-rolled puff pastry

2 Cadbury Creme Eggs, chopped into small pieces

1 egg, lightly beaten

icing sugar to dust

1. Preheat the oven to 200°C/180°C fan/gas mark 6 and line a large baking sheet with baking parchment.
2. Unroll the pastry and cut it in half lengthways so you have two long thin strips.
3. Dot the Cadbury Creme Egg pieces evenly over one of the pastry strips. Brush the edges of the pastry with a little beaten egg and place the other pastry strip on top, pressing down lightly to seal.
4. Cut the pastry into 16 short strips about 2cm wide using a sharp knife or a pizza cutter. Take each strip and twist it three or four times, then place it on the baking sheet, pressing down the ends to stop them untwisting. Repeat with the rest of the strips, leaving a gap between them on the baking sheet as they will puff up as they cook.
5. Brush each twist with a little beaten egg and then bake them in the oven for 15 minutes until they are puffed up and golden. Leave them to cool on a wire rack and dust them with icing sugar before serving.

Per serving

122 kcals	6.9g fat	3.3g sat fat	3.8g sugar	0.1g salt

CADBURY CREME EGG FRYING PAN COOKIE

Bigger is always better in our book. So crack out the frying pan for this big boy and we guarantee this gooey cookie will win over even your harshest critics.

SERVES 8
PREP TIME 15 MINS
COOKING TIME 20 MINS

150g butter, softened

175g golden caster sugar

1 egg

1 tsp vanilla extract

250g plain flour

1 tsp baking powder

3 Cadbury Creme Eggs, chopped into pieces

vanilla ice-cream, to serve (optional)

1. Preheat the oven to 190°C/170°C fan/gas mark 5. Butter a 20cm ovenproof frying pan or cast-iron skillet – or you can use a 20cm shallow cake tin.
2. Cream together the butter and sugar with a hand-held whisk until they are pale and creamy, add the egg and vanilla extract and beat again.
3. Fold in the flour and the baking powder, then add the Cadbury Creme Egg pieces and fold them into the cookie dough.
4. Spoon the dough into the frying pan and smooth it to the edges with the back of a spoon, then bake it in the oven for 20 minutes until golden.
5. Leave the cookie to rest for 10 minutes before serving it with scoops of vanilla ice-cream, if liked.

Per serving

376 kcals	18.7g fat	11.4g sat fat	32g sugar	0.1g salt

CADBURY CREME EGG AFFOGATO

Affogato good this tastes! This posh take on an ice-cream sundae is quick, easy and made even more amazing thanks to the gooey goody on top.

SERVES 2
PREP TIME 5 MINS, PLUS FREEZING

2 scoops vanilla ice-cream
2 shots hot espresso coffee
1 Cadbury Creme Egg, halved

1. Scoop the ice-cream on to a small baking sheet lined with baking parchment and freeze it for an hour, or until ready to serve – this ensures that it won't melt too quickly when you pour the coffee over it.
2. Make the two shots of espresso, put a scoop of ice-cream into each of two small serving bowls and top with half a Cadbury Creme Egg. Serve the ice-cream with the shot of coffee alongside, then pour the coffee over it and eat it immediately.

Per serving

146 kcals	4.8g fat	3.5g sat fat	21.2g sugar	0.004g salt

CADBURY CREME EGG TOASTIE

This golden brown gooey snack is the best thing since sliced bread! With just two slices, a bit of butter and a Cadbury Creme Egg, you can turn your loaf into the toast with the most!

MAKES 1 TOASTED SANDWICH
PREP TIME 1 MIN
COOKING TIME 3–4 MINS

1 Cadbury Creme Egg, chopped into pieces

2 slices medium white sliced bread

2 tsp butter

cocoa powder, for dusting

1. Switch on the sandwich toaster and wait for it to heat up, or put a non-stick frying pan over a medium heat.
2. Place the Cadbury Creme Egg pieces on a plate and microwave them for about 10 seconds, until softened, then mash them with a fork.
3. Spread butter on the outside of both pieces of bread.
4. Place one slice of bread on the sandwich toaster or in the frying pan butter side down. Put the partly-melted Cadbury Creme Egg on top of the bread, spreading it out evenly. Place the second slice of bread on top (butter side up) and close the lid of the sandwich maker, securing it in place.
5. Cook the sandwich for about 4–5 minutes until the bread is golden on the outside. If using a frying pan, turn the sandwich once, making sure both sides are golden and crisp.
6. Carefully remove the toasted sandwich and slice it diagonally in two, cutting off any excess crusts on the sides.
7. To serve, lightly dust a plate with cocoa powder and place the sandwich halves on top, slightly overlapping.

Per serving

367 kcals	15.3g fat	9.1g sat fat	28g sugar	0.5g salt

CADBURY CREME EGG CHEESECAKE SLICES

This sweet treat will be right up your street. With its buttery, biscuity base and deliciously rich, creamy top who can resist? Goo on, you know you want to.

MAKES 12 SLICES
PREP TIME 30 MINS,
PLUS OVERNIGHT CHILLING
COOKING TIME 10 MINS

300g milk chocolate digestive biscuits, crushed into fine crumbs

75g butter, melted

3 gelatine leaves

150ml double cream

500g light soft cheese

150g 0% fat Greek yoghurt

100g caster sugar

3 Cadbury Creme Eggs

1. Preheat the oven to 170°C/150°C fan/gas mark 3 and line a 20 x 24 x 4cm baking tin with non-stick baking parchment.
2. Put the biscuit crumbs into a bowl and mix them with the melted butter. Tip the mixture into the baking tin and press it down with the back of a spoon to make an even layer.
3. Bake the biscuit base for 10 minutes until it is golden. Remove the tin from the oven and place it on a wire rack to cool.
4. Put the gelatine in a small bowl, cover it with cold water and set it aside for 5 minutes to soften.
5. Heat 50ml of the cream in a small pan until it begins to bubble at the edges, then remove the pan from the heat. Squeeze the water from the gelatine then add the gelatine to the pan, stirring it into the cream until it melts.
6. Put the remaining cream, the soft cheese, yoghurt and caster sugar in a large bowl and whisk them with a hand-held mixer. Beat the mixture for 5 minutes until it is smooth and thick. Add the gelatine cream to the bowl and whisk the mixture again briefly to combine all the ingredients.
7. Spoon the cream cheese mixture over the biscuit base and smooth the surface. Leave it to chill in the fridge for at least 4 hours, or ideally overnight.
8. When you are ready to serve, cut two of the Cadbury Creme Eggs into pieces and scatter them on top. Heat the third Cadbury Creme Egg in a microwave on medium for 30 seconds. Spoon out the gooey centre and drizzle it over the cheesecake before slicing.

Per serving

375 kcals	23.7g fat	14.2g sat fat	25.5g sugar	0.5g salt

CADBURY CREME EGG CHOCOLATE BARK

There's no way you can make a dog's dinner of this one.
This melt-in-the-mouth masterpiece can be made in mere minutes
(and will be wolfed down even faster). Looks cool and makes guests drool.

SERVES 12
PREP TIME 15 MINS,
PLUS CHILLING

100g dark chocolate
100g milk chocolate
150g white chocolate
yellow food colouring
2 Cadbury Creme Eggs, chopped

1. Melt the three chocolates in separate bowls in a microwave on medium or over a saucepan of gently simmering water, making sure that the base of each bowl doesn't touch the water.
2. Line a shallow 20 x 30cm baking tin with baking parchment.
3. Spoon alternating spoonfuls of the dark and milk chocolate and half the white chocolate on to the baking parchment. Mix a few drops of yellow food colouring into the remaining white chocolate then spoon it around the other three types of chocolate. Use the end of a round-bladed knife to gently stir the different types of chocolate into each other in decorative swirls.
4. Dot the Cadbury Creme Egg pieces on top of the melted chocolate. Leave the bark to set in the fridge for an hour or two, then break it into shards.

Per serving

189 kcals	10.5g fat	6.5g sat fat	20g sugar	0.07g salt

TIP You could make chocolate eggs from the bark as an Easter gift. Before the chocolate has set completely cut egg shapes from the bark, then leave them to set. Place them in a small transparent bag and tie the top with a ribbon.

CADBURY CREME EGG MILKSHAKE

Take a break from the bake and crack into this shake
because it's udderly delicious!

SERVES 1
PREP TIME 5 MINS

1 scoop light vanilla ice-cream
1 Cadbury Mini Creme Egg,
chopped into pieces
150ml semi-skimmed milk

1. Put the ice-cream, most of the Cadbury Creme Egg pieces
   and the milk into a blender and whizz until smooth.
2. Pour the milkshake into a tall glass and serve it immediately,
   topped with the last few pieces of chopped Cadbury Creme Egg.

Per serving

131 kcals	4.8g fat	3.1g sat fat	16g sugar	0.12g salt

TIP Add a banana to the blender to make an extra-thick milkshake,
or try some strawberries for a splash of colour.

CADBURY CREME EGG ROCKY ROAD BARS

These chunky chocolate concoctions will set you on the road to greatness.
Marshmallows – good. Biscuit pieces – great. Dark chocolate – delicious.
Mini Cadbury Creme Eggs – now you're talking!

MAKES 24
PREP TIME 15 MINS,
PLUS COOLING

75g butter

220g dark chocolate, broken
into small pieces

2 tbsp golden syrup

150g digestive biscuits,
roughly broken

50g mini marshmallows

180g dried apricots, chopped

1 x 89g bag Cadbury Mini Creme
Eggs

1. Line a 20 x 35cm baking tin with baking parchment.
2. Place a large, heatproof bowl over a saucepan of boiling
   water, making sure that the water does not touch the bottom
   of the bowl, and melt the butter and chocolate together until
   they are smooth. Stir in the golden syrup.
3. Mix the digestive biscuit pieces with the apricots and mini
   marshmallows. Add to the chocolate and mix to combine
   them all thoroughly. Make sure everything is well coated in
   chocolate or the mixture won't stick together.
4. Press the mixture into the tin using the back of a spatula or
   wooden spoon, then push in the whole Cadbury Mini Creme
   Eggs. Space them evenly apart so there will be an egg in each
   piece. Chill in the fridge for at least 2 hours to set.
5. Use a sharp knife to slice the mixture into 24 squares. Store
   the bars in the fridge to keep them as solid as possible.

Per serving

143 kcals	7g fat	4.1g sat fat	13.5g sugar	0.1g salt

CADBURY CREME EGG, BANANAS & CUSTARD

These super-simple mini desserts are a cracking way to end the day. Whip 'em up in no time and eat 'em even quicker. This Cadbury Creme Egg twist on tradition will tickle your taste buds.

SERVES 6
PREP TIME 15 MINS

600ml semi-skimmed milk
6 egg yolks
50g caster sugar
1 tbsp cornflour
1 tsp vanilla bean paste
4 small bananas
2 Cadbury Creme Eggs, cut into 18 pieces

1. Heat the milk in a saucepan until it is just beginning to bubble at the edges, then remove the pan from the heat.
2. Put the egg yolks, sugar, cornflour and vanilla bean paste into a large bowl and whisk them together until they are smooth. Slowly add the hot milk to the bowl, whisking as you pour, then return the custard to the pan and set it over a gentle heat.
3. Slowly cook the custard, stirring continuously for about 10 minutes until it thickens enough to coat the back of the spoon – when you drag your finger across the spoon it should leave a path.
4. Peel and slice the bananas into six bowls, divide the custard between them, top with the Cadbury Creme Egg pieces and serve immediately.

TIP Don't throw away overripe bananas; freeze them to give you a ready supply for banana bread or smoothies. To freeze bananas, peel them and cut them in half, then place the halves on a piece of baking parchment and freeze for 3–4 hours until they are solid. Transfer to a freezer bag. They will last 2–3 months.

Per serving

259 kcals	8.2g fat	3.8g sat fat	34g sugar	0.1g salt

CADBURY CREME EGG POPCORN

Try this as a Saturday night snack or serve it at a sleepover! Gooey chocolatey goodness dripped over delicious home-made popcorn gets five stars from us.

SERVES 8
PREP TIME 10 MINS

1 tbsp vegetable oil

70g popcorn kernels

50g butter

2 Cadbury Creme Eggs, chopped into pieces

1. Heat the oil in a large saucepan, add the popcorn kernels and place the lid on the pan. Cook over a medium heat until the corn stops popping, shaking the pan every now and then.
2. Melt the butter and pour it into a large bowl. Add the cooked popcorn, stir to coat it in butter then add the Cadbury Creme Egg pieces. Stir gently to melt the chocolate slightly and serve immediately.

Per serving

139 kcals	8.7g fat	4.4g sat fat	7g sugar	0.03g salt

TIP To make a quick sweet and savoury snack use lightly salted microwave popcorn – it usually cooks in just 2–3 minutes in a microwave! Then coat as above.

CADBURY CREME EGG SOURDOUGH TOASTS

How do you like your eggs in the morning? We like ours eggstra gooey and served on soft sourdough. So go bananas and raise a toast to your taste buds at breakfast, lunch or dinner.

SERVES 4
PREP TIME 15 MINS

2 Cadbury Creme Eggs, chopped

25g butter

2 bananas

4 slices sourdough bread

40g pecans, chopped (optional)

1. Melt two-thirds of the the Cadbury Creme Egg pieces with the butter in a small saucepan over a low heat, or in a bowl in a microwave for 30–40 seconds on medium heat.

2. Remove the pan from the heat and beat the mixture with a wooden spoon until it is smooth and glossy.

3. Slice the bananas, then toast the slices of bread. Spread the toast pieces with Cadbury Creme Egg butter and top them with banana slices and chopped nuts, if using. Add a quarter of the remaining Cadbury Creme Egg pieces to each slice and serve immediately.

Per serving

250 kcals	9g fat	5g sat fat	20g sugar	1g salt

CADBURY CREME EGG HOT CHOCOLATE

Chase away the winter goos with this tasty Cadbury Creme Egg cuppa!
A sweet way to make your next hot chocolate that eggstra bit special.

SERVES 1
PREP TIME 5 MINS

1 tsp cocoa powder, plus extra
for sprinkling

165ml skimmed milk

½ Cadbury Creme Egg, cut
into pieces

You will need a small electric whisk

1. Put the cocoa powder and a dash of milk into a microwaveable jug or a small saucepan. Stir until you have a paste, then add the rest of the milk.
2. Put the jug into a microwave and heat on medium–high until steam begins to rise – about 90 seconds, or heat the pan gently over a medium heat for 1–2 minutes.
3. Take out the jug, add the Cadbury Creme Egg pieces and mix until they are melted. If using a saucepan, take it off the heat before adding the Cadbury Creme Egg pieces and mixing them until melted. Pour the hot chocolate into a cup and froth it with an electric whisk for about 30 seconds. Sprinkle a small quantity of cocoa powder on top and serve.

Per serving

153 kcals	3.7g fat	2g sat fat	19.2g sugar	0.3g salt

CADBURY CREME EGG FONGOO

Grab your kitschest bowl and create a Cadbury Creme Egg twist on a continental classic. Break out the breadsticks and sort yourself some strawberries to enjoy this eggstraordinary treat.

SERVES 2
PREP TIME 10 MINS
COOKING TIME 10 MINS

60ml single cream

1 Cadbury Creme Egg, chopped into pieces

25g milk chocolate, broken into small pieces

4 mini breadsticks

6 strawberries, washed and halved

1. Put the cream in a glass bowl over a saucepan of gently simmering water, making sure that the bottom of the bowl does not touch the water.
2. When the cream is warm stir in the Cadbury Creme Egg pieces and the chocolate and continue to stir until they have melted completely.
3. Transfer the mixture to a dipping cup and serve it warm alongside the breadsticks and strawberries.

Per serving

239 kcals	12.8g fat	7.8g sat fat	22.9g sugar	0.1g salt

CADBURY CREME EGG WAFFLES

Pancakes are great, but what has more goo-gathering ability than a perfectly pocketed waffle? Goo on ... waffle you waiting for?

MAKES 16
PREP TIME 5 MINS
COOKING TIME 6–7 MINS
PER WAFFLE

385ml skimmed milk

3 eggs

4 tbsp olive oil

1 tsp vanilla extract

¾ tsp baking powder

¾ tsp salt

320g plain flour

16 tsp light chocolate sauce

16 Cadbury Mini Creme Eggs, chopped into small pieces

You will need a waffle iron

1. Put the milk, eggs, oil and vanilla extract in a jug and whisk them together to combine.
2. In a large bowl, mix the baking powder, salt and flour. Gradually whisk the wet ingredients into the dry. The mixture should be quite thick. Leave it to rest for 30 minutes.
3. Preheat the waffle iron for 3–4 minutes, then pour a ladle full of batter onto the centre of the iron and away from the edges to form a round waffle. Cook the waffle for 6–7 minutes, or until golden and then remove it. Drizzle a teaspoon of chocolate sauce on top and a few pieces of chopped Cadbury Mini Creme Egg. Continue cooking waffles until you have used up all the batter.

Per serving

193 kcals	7.3g fat	2.2g sat fat	10.6g sugar	0.3g salt

INDEX

D